Houghton
Mifflin
Harcourt

PERFORMANCE ASSESSMENT

7

Cover and Title Page Photo Credit: ©imagewerks/Getty Images

Printed in the U.S.A.

ISBN 978-0-544-56934-8

12   0690   21 20 19

4500788513   A B C D E F G

Approaching Performance Assessments with Confidence

By Carol Jago

In order to get good at anything, you need to practice. Whether the goal is to improve your jump shot, level up in a video game, or make the cut in band tryouts, success requires repeated practice on the court, computer, and field. The same is true of reading and writing. The only way to get good at them is by reading and writing.

Malcolm Gladwell estimates in his book *Outliers* that mastering a skill requires about 10,000 hours of dedicated practice. He argues that individuals who are outstanding in their field have one thing in common—many, many hours of working at it. Gladwell claims that success is less dependent on innate talent than it is on practice. Now I'm pretty sure that I could put in 10,000 hours at a ballet studio and still be a terrible dancer, but I agree with Gladwell that, "Practice isn't the thing you do once you're good. It's the thing you do that makes you good."

Not just any kind of practice will help you master a skill, though. Effective practice needs to focus on improvement. That is why this series of reading and writing tasks begins with a model of the kind of reading and writing you are working towards, then takes you through practice exercises, and finally invites you to perform the skills you have practiced.

Once through the cycle is only the beginning. You will want to repeat the process many times over until close reading, supporting claims with evidence, and crafting a compelling essay is something you approach with confidence. Notice that I didn't say "with ease." I wish it were otherwise, but in my experience as a teacher and as an author, writing well is never easy.

The work is worth the effort. Like a star walking out on the stage, you put your trust in the hours you've invested in practice to result in thundering applause. To our work together!

Unit 1 Argumentative Essay
Investigating the Unknown

STEP 1 ANALYZE THE MODEL

Should we celebrate Columbus Day?

Read Source Materials

NEWSPAPER EDITORIAL
The Columbus Day Dilemma: To Celebrate or
Not to Celebrate?   The Holiday Blogger!   4

NEWSPAPER EDITORIAL
Let's Celebrate Indigenous Peoples Day   The San Francisco Bugle   5

STUDENT MODEL
The Start of Something New   Alison Rodriguez   6

STEP 2 PRACTICE THE TASK

*Should people have the right to claim territory
in outer space?*

Read Source Materials

BLOG
Red Planet Realty   Edith Rivera   10

BIOGRAPHY
Elon Musk: Private Spaceflight Pioneer   Paolo Rizzi   11

ADVERTISEMENT
Everybody's Going to Be a Space Pioneer   12

NEWSPAPER ARTICLE
Can You Own Land in Outer Space?   Teresa Anjou   13

Write an Argumentative Essay

*Should people have the right to claim territory
in outer space?*
     16

STEP 3 PERFORM THE TASK

Do people have the right to rescue services when they put themselves at risk?

Read Source Materials

RADIO INTERVIEW
Helicopter Rescues Increasing on Everest   Robert Siegel   22

INFORMATIONAL ARTICLE
Why Everest?   Guy Moreau   25

NEWSPAPER ARTICLE
Ranger Killed During Rescue of
Climbers on Mount Rainier   Janice Winfield   28

Write an Argumentative Essay

*Do people have the right to rescue services
when they put themselves at risk?*   31

Unit 2 Informative Essay
Things Change

STEP 1 ANALYZE THE MODEL

Why does our knowledge of the universe change over time?

Read Source Materials

INSTRUCTIONAL ESSAY
Starting Strong   36

STUDENT MODEL
A Universe of Knowledge   Anita Brown   38

STUDENT MODEL
Planet X or Dwarf Planet?   Joseph Keegan   40

STEP 2 PRACTICE THE TASK

How is the presence of Burmese pythons changing the Everglades?

Read Source Materials

INFORMATIONAL ARTICLE
Burmese Python: Not the Ideal Pet · Matt Piven · 44

NEWSPAPER ARTICLE
Florida's Python Hunt · Andrew Ng · 45

ADVERTISEMENT
Python Challenge · 46

BLOG
Burmese Python: The Ecosystem Challenge · EcoEchoes · 47

Write an Informative Essay

How is the presence of Burmese pythons changing the Everglades? · 50

STEP 3 PERFORM THE TASK

Why does scientific knowledge change over time?

Read Source Materials

MAGAZINE ARTICLE
The Half-Life of Facts · Samuel Arbesman · 56

NEWSPAPER ARTICLE
The Food Pyramid and Why It Changed · William Neuman · 58

INFORMATIONAL TEXT
The Explosion in What We Know About Life Forms · Alan Cochev · 60

Write an Informative Essay

Why does scientific knowledge change over time? · 65

© Houghton Mifflin Harcourt Publishing Company • Image Credits: ©lunatic67/Shutterstock; ©Albert J. Copley/Photodisc/Getty Images

Unit 3 Literary Analysis
Making Choices

STEP 1 ANALYZE THE MODEL

How do I analyze a poem?

Read Source Materials

BIOGRAPHY
Robert Frost: The Poet and His Craft   Lee Ann Windsor   70

POEM
Stopping by Woods on a Snowy Evening   Robert Frost   71

STUDENT MODEL
Interpreting Sound and Symbol in Frost's
"Stopping by Woods on a Snowy Evening"   Keisha Roberts   72

STEP 2 PRACTICE THE TASK

How does an author develop a theme?

Read Source Materials

INFORMATIVE ESSAY
What Is a . . . Universal Theme   Doris Sato   76

FOLK TALE
The Old Grandfather and His Little Grandson   *retold by* Leo Tolstoy   78

POEM
Abuelito Who   Sandra Cisneros   79

Write a Literary Analysis

*What universal theme is expressed in the folk
tale and the poem?*   82

STEP 3 PERFORM THE TASK

What techniques do authors use to create characters?

Read Source Materials

INFORMATIVE ESSAY
Characters: The Human Experience   John Leggett   88

SHORT STORY
The Open Window   Saki (H. H. Munro)   90

Write a Literary Analysis

*How does Saki develop the characters of Nuttel
and Vera in "The Open Window"?*   95

Unit 4 Mixed Practice
On Your Own

TASK 1 ARGUMENTATIVE ESSAY
RESEARCH SIMULATION

Read Source Materials

INFORMATIONAL ARTICLE
What Is a Strike?   Sharon Blumenstein   103

NEWSPAPER ARTICLE
New York School Bus Strike: Sign of National
Pressure on Unions   Stacy Teicher Khadaroo   104

Anchor Text
INFORMATIONAL ARTICLE
Why Is it Rare for Public Sector Workers
to Go on Strike   Mia Lewis   105

Write an Argumentative Essay   108

TASK 2 INFORMATIVE ESSAY
RESEARCH SIMULATION

Read Source Materials

INFORMATIONAL ARTICLE
Past and Present: The Florida Everglades   Tobey Haskell   113

Anchor Text
NEWSPAPER ARTICLE
Can We Fix the Water Supply?   Caleb Hughes   115

NEWSPAPER ARTICLE
Water Quality Nearly Halts Everglades
Restoration   Robin Martelli   117

Write an Informative Essay   120

TASK 3 LITERARY ANALYSIS

Read Source Materials

POEM
Inside a Poem   Eve Merriam   125

POEM
Introduction to Poetry   Billy Collins   126

Write a Literary Analysis   129

Investigating the Unknown

Argumentative Essay

STEP 1

ANALYZE THE MODEL

Evaluate an argumentative essay about whether we should celebrate Columbus Day.

STEP 2

PRACTICE THE TASK

Write an argumentative essay on people's right to claim territory in outer space.

STEP 3

PERFORM THE TASK

Write an argumentative essay for or against the rescue of individuals who put themselves at risk.

Disagreement is a part of everyday life. Interacting with others—friends, neighbors, relatives, strangers—can sometimes lead to disagreements. Arguing, giving your reasons for your stance on an issue, and explaining your point of view, can be challenging on a person-to-person level.

The argumentative essay, on the other hand, is a more formally constructed argument.

IN THIS UNIT you will learn how to write an argumentative essay that is based on your close reading and analysis of several relevant sources. You will learn a step-by-step approach to stating a precise claim—and then organize your essay to support your claim in a clear and logical way.

Should we celebrate Columbus Day?

You will read:

▶ **TWO NEWSPAPER EDITORIALS**

The Columbus Day Dilemma: To Celebrate or Not to Celebrate?

Let's Celebrate Indigenous Peoples Day

You will analyze:

▶ **A STUDENT MODEL**
The Start of Something New

Source Materials for Step 1

The newspaper editorials on these two pages were used by Mr. George's student, Alison Rodriguez, as sources for her essay, "The Start of Something New." As you read, make notes in the side columns and underline information that you find useful.

NOTES

The Columbus Day Dilemma:
TO CELEBRATE OR NOT TO CELEBRATE?

from The Holiday Blogger!

Columbus Day has to be one of our most controversial holidays. To some people, it's a way to celebrate the daring achievements of the explorer who "discovered" America. They say Columbus was the founder of the first permanent European settlement in the New World and that his arrival marked the start of recorded history in America. Plus, it's a day to celebrate the heritage of 26 million Italian Americans—the nation's fifth largest ethnic group. Fantastic! Let's party!

But wait—it seems not everyone agrees even on that much. First of all, many believe that Vikings started a colony on Newfoundland, Canada, hundreds of years before Columbus arrived in the Caribbean. Secondly, there was certainly writing in the Americas before Columbus arrived (Mayan hieroglyphics, for example), just not writing that Columbus could read! And of course, the very idea that someone could "discover" a well-inhabited continent is kind of crazy. As for celebrating Italian Americans—why doesn't every ethnic group have a federal holiday?

Perhaps we should agree to disagree and let each person decide if he or she is going to celebrate this controversial holiday or not. Meanwhile, let's look out for another day that represents something we can all get behind!

Let's Celebrate Indigenous Peoples Day

The San Francisco Bugle

Columbus Day—a federal holiday since 1937—commemorates the famous explorer's arrival in the New World way back in 1492.

The problem is, not everyone wants to celebrate the man who opened the Americas to European colonization. Just think about all the misery that followed: land grabbing, enslavement, disease, death, and the near extinction of native peoples. One spokesman for Native Americans in the U.S. summed it up this way: "Columbus doesn't deserve parades and holidays; this should be a national day of mourning." Continuing to celebrate Columbus Day is so insensitive, it's embarrassing.

Perhaps there is a way to take this lemon of a holiday and make lemonade by turning it on its head. Why not celebrate Indigenous Peoples Day instead? Instead of a day commemorating one explorer—or a day of private mourning and sadness for those who were killed—we could have a day of tribute and celebration for the survivors and the culture that they continue to uphold and strengthen into the current day.

The second Monday of October could be a day to learn about the Native Americans who were here when Europeans first arrived—and discover and salute the vibrant and developing cultures of all of today's indigenous peoples. Now that's worth celebrating!

Discuss and Decide

You've read two sources about celebrating Columbus Day. Without going any further, discuss the question: Should we celebrate Columbus Day?

Analyze a Student Model for Step 1

Read Alison's argumentative essay closely. The red side notes are the comments that her teacher, Mr. George, wrote.

Christopher Columbus

Alison Rodriguez
Mr. George
English 7
September 29

The Start of Something New

Interesting hook.

Don't be shocked, but Columbus didn't discover America! How we look at Columbus Day has changed over the years. In 1492, a man who never realized that he had not found a route to India changed the future of our world forever. His voyage began the recognition of the Americas by Europe. That is something worth celebrating.

The issue and your claim are clear.

Valid reason that supports your claim with evidence.

Because of Columbus, other Europeans started coming to the New World. The Spanish conquistadors came searching for gold. They brought with them their Christian faith and their language. Would Latin America be Latin, if it wasn't for Columbus?

Good transition.

Later, settlers came for a better life and greater freedom, a fresh start in a new place. Jamestown, Plymouth Rock, and even New York were settled because of the interest sparked by Columbus' travels. The people who came brought their hopes, dreams, skills, and knowledge. They established colonies, which became villages, which grew into towns and cities. New York might be a different place today if Columbus had never sailed.

You make an excellent point!

Alison, I'm not sure that Halloween warrants a day off!

That Columbus Day is a school holiday is another reason for celebration. We really have too many school days, and a nice three-day weekend in October is really appreciated. Since we don't get a day off for Halloween, Columbus Day is a fair trade.

1. Analyze   2. Practice   3. Perform

Columbus Day is controversial, besides the fact that Columbus didn't discover America. Many different tribes of indigenous people lived in the Americas before 1492. Columbus enslaved the Taíno people he found living on the islands when he landed. We should be sensitive to the feelings of Native Americans, who were mistreated by white men for many years beginning with Columbus. But that doesn't mean we can't honor Columbus and other Italian Americans who made important contributions to our country and deserve to be recognized.

On Columbus Day we should consider our past and the debt we owe to adventurers. Columbus took a big risk sailing to places unknown. He had no way of knowing how his voyage would affect the world. We should recognize and celebrate Columbus Day.

You identified an opposing claim and responded with logical evidence.

Convincing evidence and smooth flow from beginning to end.

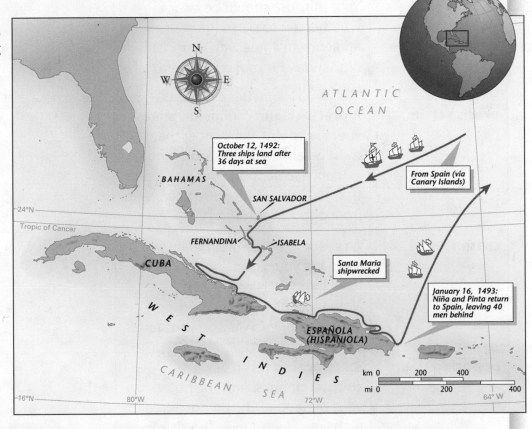

The map above shows a portion of the route Christopher Columbus took on his first voyage in 1492. He found the Taíno people living on the group of islands known today as the Bahamas.

Discuss and Decide

Did Alison's essay convince you that Columbus Day should be celebrated? If so, cite the most compelling text evidence in her essay.

Terminology of Argumentative Texts

Read each word and explanation. Then look back at Alison Rodriguez's argumentative essay and find an example to complete the chart.

Term	Explanation	Example from Alison's Essay
audience	The **audience** for your argument is a group of people that you want to convince. As you develop your argument, consider your audience's knowledge level and concerns.	
purpose	The **purpose** for writing an argument is to sway the audience. Your purpose should be clear, whether it is to persuade your audience to agree with your claim, or to motivate your audience to take some action.	
precise claim	A **precise claim** confidently states your viewpoint. Remember that you must be able to find reasons and evidence to support your claim, and that you must distinguish your claim from opposing claims.	
reason	A **reason** is a statement that supports your claim. (You should have more than one reason.) Note that you will need to supply evidence for each reason you state.	
opposing claim	An **opposing claim** or **counterclaim**, shares the point of view of people who do not agree with your claim. Opposing claims must be fairly presented with evidence.	

1. Analyze   2. Practice   3. Perform

Should people have the right to claim territory in outer space?

You will read:

▶ **A BLOG**
Red Planet Realty

▶ **A BIOGRAPHY**
Elon Musk: Private Spaceflight Pioneer

▶ **AN ADVERTISEMENT**
Everybody's Going to Be a Space Pioneer

▶ **A NEWSPAPER ARTICLE**
Can You Own Land in Outer Space?

You will write:

▶ **AN ARGUMENTATIVE ESSAY**
Should people have the right to claim territory in outer space?

Source Materials for Step 2

AS YOU READ Read the blog, the biography, the magazine advertisement, and the newspaper article. Think about the information contained in the sources. Annotate the sources with notes that help you decide where you stand on the issue: Should people have the right to claim territory in outer space?

Source 1: Blog

Red Planet Realty

Enter your email address:

Subscribe me!

SEARCH

To all my blog followers:

Don't be left behind on Earth. Stake your claim to your very own piece of Mars today. As the only authorized realtor for property on the red planet, I am pleased to make the first public offering. Land on Mars is free! Choose your own square-mile parcel of land from a grid map. Parcels will be awarded on a first-come, first-served basis, with only one to a customer. Transportation to and from Mars will not be provided.

A full-color brochure and a grid map are available for the low cost of $29.99.

P.S.—If you really send money, I'll include an asteroid belt free of charge!

Close Read

What assumptions does Red Planet Realty make about its online followers? What details give you that impression?

_____

_____

ELON MUSK
Private Spaceflight Pioneer

In Elon Musk's view, a space colony on Mars is not a matter of *if!* It's a matter of *when!* His company, Space X, has contracted with the government of the United States to supply the transportation of cargo to and from the International Space Station (ISS).

Space X's first of 12 NASA resupply missions to the ISS, using Space X's Dragon capsule, took place in October, 2012. The cargo supply mission was deemed a huge success. Since the retirement of the space shuttle fleet in 2011, NASA has relied on other countries, namely Russia, to send cargo and astronauts to the space station and back. Private companies can now handle the cargo portion of that job and will someday carry astronauts as well.

Elon Musk, born in South Africa in 1971, loved computers as a child and by the age of 12, had written the code for a video game called *Blastar*, which he sold

Elon Musk, inventor, space pioneer, and entrepreneur

for a profit. He started his first company at 24, and in 1999 he invented a method of securely transferring money on the Internet, which later became PayPal, a large global payment transfer provider. He started Space X in 2002, and in 2004 he cofounded Tesla Motors, an electric car company.

Mr. Musk's vision for the Mars space colony includes a price tag of $500,000 per person. Currently Musk is working on a prototype rocket for the mission, called *Grasshopper*. He sees the colony program as collaboration between government and private enterprise that would cost a lot of money (a whopping—$36 billion!) to establish. "That was true of the English colonies [in the Americas]," Musk said. "It took significant expense to get things started. But once there are regular Mars flights, you can get the cost down to half a million dollars for someone to move to Mars. Then I think there are enough people who would buy that to have it be a reasonable business case."

Discuss and Decide

Compare Sources 1 and 2. Which text makes space colonization seem like a realistic possibility? Cite text evidence in your response.

Everybody's Going to Be a Space Pioneer

For application and inquiries, visit
www.1way2mars.com

WHAT ABOUT YOU?

For only 5 payments of $99,999.99 you can travel to the

OFFICAL SPACE PIONEER OUTPOST

in beautiful Red Rock City, Mars

WHAT ARE YOU WAITING FOR?

This is a TRULY out-of this-world experience! An acre of prime Mars real estate will be yours upon arrival!

- Return trip not included.
- Meals not included.
- Classes in Mars survival techniques are extra.
- Void where prohibited.

Discuss and Decide

Evaluate the advertisement for becoming a space pioneer. What other information would you want to know before you agreed to go?

1. Analyze   2. Practice   3. Perform

Source 4: Newspaper Article

Miami Herald

Can You Own Land in Outer Space?

by Teresa Anjou   December 2, 2012

What if you could own property on the Moon or Mars? Sounds like science fiction? The Space Settlement Prize Act is proposed federal legislation that would allow private companies to finance and build permanent settlements on the Moon and Mars. Many believe that giving people the ability to purchase and sell property rights in space would allow for the development of the last frontier—space.

In 1967, the Outer Space Treaty was signed by one hundred countries, including the United States. The treaty bars countries from laying claim to the Moon and other planets. No mention, however, was made in the treaty about personal ownership. In 1979 another treaty, known as the Moon Treaty, was proposed. It was never ratified by any of the countries that had explored space. Backers of the Space Settlement Prize Act believe that this created a "loophole." They believe that the U.S. government can recognize ownership of land in outer space.

Why would a company want to go to the trouble of claiming the Moon, Mars, or even an asteroid? Firstly, there may be valuable minerals in these locations. Secondly, as the cost of spaceflight comes down, space tourism could be a moneymaking venture.

Some legal experts say the loophole doesn't exist. A section of the Outer Space Treaty requires that nations be held responsible for any settlement activities of their citizens. That would preclude any effort to uphold property claims.

Discuss and Decide

What questions does the newspaper article raise about outer space real estate ventures? Cite text evidence in your response.

Respond to Questions on Step 2 Sources

These questions will help you analyze the sources you've read. Use your notes and refer to the sources in order to answer the questions. Your answers to these questions will help you write your essay.

1 Evaluate the sources. Is the evidence from one source more credible than the evidence from another source? When you evaluate the credibility of a source, consider the expertise of the author and/or the organization responsible for the information. Record your reasons in the chart.

Source	Credible?	Reasons
Blog Red Planet Realty		
Biography Elon Musk: Private Spaceflight Pioneer		
Advertisement Everybody's Going to Be a Space Pioneer		
Newspaper Article Can You Own Land in Outer Space?		

2 **Prose Constructed-Response** Both the biography and the newspaper article mention owning property beyond Earth. According to the sources, is space travel more realistic for individuals or organizations? Cite text evidence in your response.

_____

_____

3 **Prose Constructed-Response** According to "Can You Own Land in Outer Space?" is it legal for individuals to own land in space at the present time? Cite text evidence in your response.

_____

_____

Types of Evidence

Every reason you offer to support the central claim of your argument must be backed up by evidence. It is useful to think ahead about evidence when you are preparing to write an argument. If there is no evidence to support your claim, you will need to revise your claim. The evidence you provide must be relevant, or related to your claim. It must also be sufficient. Sufficient evidence is both clear and varied.

Use this chart to help you choose different types of evidence to support your reasons.

Types of Evidence	What Does It Look Like?
Anecdotes: personal examples or stories that illustrate a point	**Biography** "Elon Musk, born in South Africa in 1971, loved computers as a child . . ."
Commonly accepted beliefs: ideas that most people share	**Newspaper Article** "Many believe that giving people the ability to purchase and sell property rights in space would allow for the development of the last frontier—space."
Examples: specific instances or illustrations of a general idea	**Newspaper Article** "A section of the Outer Space Treaty requires that nations be held responsible for any settlement activities of their citizens."
Expert opinion: statement made by an authority on the subject	**Biography** "But once there are regular Mars flights, you can get the cost down to half a million dollars for someone to move to Mars."
Facts: statements that can be proven true, such as statistics or other numerical information	**Newspaper Article** "In 1967, the Outer Space Treaty was signed by one hundred countries, including the United States."

Write an argumentative essay to answer the question: Should people have the right to claim territory in outer space?

Planning and Prewriting

Before you draft your essay, complete some important planning steps.

Claim ➡ Reasons ➡ Evidence

 You may prefer to do your planning on a computer.

Make a Precise Claim

1. Should people be able to own property in outer space?

yes ☐   no ☐

2. Review the evidence on pages 10–13. Do the sources support your position?

yes ☐   no ☐

3. If you answered *no* to Question 2, you can either change your position or do additional research to find supporting evidence.

4. State your claim. It should be precise. It should contain the issue and your position on the issue.

> **Issue:** People's right to claim territory in outer space.
>
> **Your position on the issue:** _____
>
> **Your precise claim:** _____

State Reasons

Next, gather support for your claim. Identify several valid reasons that justify your position.

Reason 1	Reason 2	Reason 3

Find Evidence

You have identified reasons that support your claim. Summarize your reasons in the chart below. Then complete the chart by identifying evidence that supports your reasons.

Relevant Evidence: The evidence you plan to use must be *relevant* to your argument. That is, it should directly and factually support your position.

Sufficient Evidence: Additionally, your evidence must be *sufficient* to make your case. That is, you need to provide enough evidence to convince others.

Short Summary of Reasons	Evidence
Reason 1	Relevant? _____ Sufficient? _____
Reason 2	Relevant? _____ Sufficient? _____
Reason 3	Relevant? _____ Sufficient? _____

Finalize Your Plan

Whether you are writing your essay at home or working in a timed situation at school, it is important to have a plan. You will save time and create a more organized, logical essay by planning the structure before you start writing.

Use your responses on pages 16–17, as well as your close reading notes, to complete the graphic organizer.

▶ Think about how you will grab your reader's attention with an interesting fact or anecdote.

▶ Identify the issue and your position.

▶ State your precise claim.
▶ List the likely opposing claim and how you will counter it.

▶ Restate your claim.

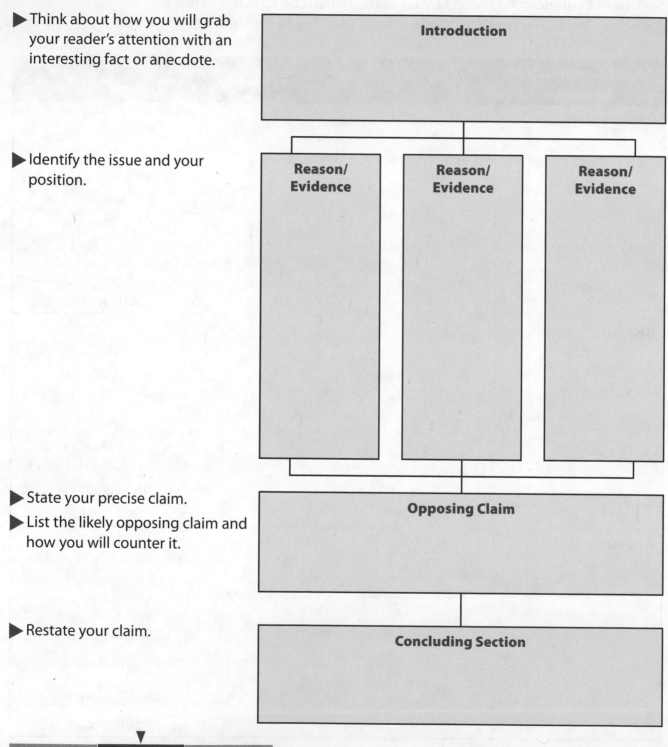

Introduction

Reason/ Evidence

Reason/ Evidence

Reason/ Evidence

Opposing Claim

Concluding Section

Draft Your Essay

As you write, think about:

▶ **Audience:** Your teacher

▶ **Purpose:** Demonstrate your understanding of the specific requirements of an argumentative essay.

▶ **Style:** Use a formal and objective tone that isn't defensive.

▶ **Transitions:** Use words, such as *furthermore* or *another reason*, to create cohesion, or flow.

Revise

Use the checklist below to guide your analysis.

Revision Checklist: Self Evaluation

 If you drafted your essay on the computer, you may wish to print it out so that you can more easily evaluate it.

Ask Yourself	Tips	Revision Strategies
1. Does the introduction grab the audience's attention and include a precise claim?	Draw a wavy line under the attention-grabbing text. Bracket the claim.	Add an attention grabber. Add a claim or rework the existing one to make it more precise.
2. Do at least two valid reasons support the claim? Is each reason supported by relevant and sufficient evidence?	Underline each reason. Circle each piece of evidence, and draw an arrow to the reason it supports.	Add reasons or revise existing ones to make them more valid. Add relevant evidence to ensure that your support is sufficient.
3. Do transitions create cohesion and link related parts of the argument?	Put a star next to each transition.	Add words, phrases, or clauses to connect related ideas that lack transitions.
4. Are the reasons in the order that is most persuasive?	Number the reasons in the margin, ranking them by their strength and effectiveness.	Rearrange the reasons into a more logical order, such as order of importance.
5. Are opposing claims fairly acknowledged and refuted?	Put a plus sign by any sentence that addresses an opposing claim.	Add sentences that identify and address those opposing claims.
6. Does the concluding section restate the claim?	Put a box around the restatement of your claim.	Add a sentence that restates your claim.

Revision Checklist: Peer Review

Exchange your essay with a classmate, or read it aloud to your partner. As you read and comment on your classmate's essay, focus on logic, organization, and evidence—not on whether you agree with the author's claim. Help each other identify parts of the draft that need strengthening, reworking, or a new approach.

What To Look For	Notes for My Partner
1. Does the introduction grab the audience's attention and include a precise claim?	
2. Do at least two valid reasons support the claim? Is each reason supported by relevant and sufficient evidence?	
3. Do transitions create cohesion and link related parts of the argument?	
4. Are the reasons in the order that is most persuasive?	
5. Are opposing claims fairly acknowledged and refuted?	
6. Does the concluding section restate the claim?	

Edit

Edit your essay to correct spelling, grammar, and punctuation errors.

1. Analyze   2. Practice   3. Perform

Do people have the right to rescue services when they put themselves at risk?

You will read:

▶ **A RADIO INTERVIEW**
Helicopter Rescues Increasing on Everest

▶ **AN INFORMATIONAL ARTICLE**
Why Everest?

▶ **A NEWSPAPER ARTICLE**
Ranger Killed During Rescue of Climbers on Mount Rainier

You will write:

▶ **AN ARGUMENTATIVE ESSAY**
Do people have the right to rescue services when they put themselves at risk?

Helicopter Rescues Increasing on Everest

ROBERT SIEGEL, HOST:

On Mount Everest, the climbing season is at its peak. And that means that if clear conditions hold, hundreds will attempt to scale the mountain this weekend alone. Suppose you wanted to climb the world's highest peak. Would it alter your decision if you knew that rescue was just a phone call, and a helicopter ride, away? Well, it turns out that helicopter rescues have been increasingly common in the mountains of Nepal. And that has raised lots of questions about risk-taking—not just for climbers but for pilots, too.

10 Nick Heil has written about this in the May issue of Outside magazine. Welcome to the program.

NICK HEIL: Nice to be here.

SIEGEL: You write that helicopters were once a last resort in the Himalayas, but I gather that's not the case anymore.

HEIL: It's not. There's been sort of the recent arrival of some powerful, new, lightweight helicopters that are able to operate at very high altitudes reliably. And they're becoming increasingly common throughout the Himalayas, in Nepal.

SIEGEL: You describe a terrible accident in which a helicopter
20 managed to evacuate one of two climbers. The helicopter could only take one climber. Is that typical of these crafts?

HEIL: It is at these kinds of altitudes. The accident that I describe in the beginning of the story, is on a peak called Ama Dablam. And the helicopter flies up to about 19,000 feet and, you know, the air at this altitude is very thin. So it requires a helicopter to utilize more power to stay aloft up there. So, you know, you can imagine, if you add weight, it's going to lose lift. So in this case, they could only bring one climber at a time. And they got one climber off, and they crashed attempting to

30 rescue the second man.

SIEGEL: How common is it to see helicopters in the skies around Everest? If you were at base camp, would you see one go by once a day, or every hour; how frequently?

HEIL: What I'm hearing now is that at the peak of the climbing season, you might see as many as four or five helicopter flights into Everest base camp in a given day. Now, I don't think that's the standard rule, but they're—certainly—more and more common up there; you know, flying trekkers in and out, flying climbers in and out.

40 **SIEGEL:** Is part of the issue here that these rescue choppers give climbers a false—or at least, a rather expensive—sense of security, and that makes them more willing to take risks?

HEIL: If you talk to professional or expert climbers, I think they're quick to sort of dismiss the fact that they might be influenced by the safety net of a helicopter being available for them. But, you know, it's hard not to believe that notion isn't in the back of somebody's mind, when they're up there in those mountains.

SIEGEL: You suggest that there might be—at least, in part—a
50 profit motive contributing to the increased use of helicopters there. How does that work?

Close Read

Why might expert climbers say that the presence of a helicopter would not influence them? Cite text evidence to support your inference.

_____

_____

HEIL: Well, the helicopter companies are privately owned and operated so it's—you know, they have to lay out quite a bit of money. I mean, these machines, the B3s, cost about $2 million apiece, and they're quite expensive to operate. So there's a lot of pressure to keep the helicopters flying and working, in order to bring in money—you know, both to pay the bill for this machine, but also to make a profit. So they're looking for opportunities to, you know, get people out, fly people in, maybe 60 bring supplies somewhere; that kind of thing.

SIEGEL: What have you heard from pilots about the difficulties of piloting a helicopter that high up?

HEIL: Well, the risks are certainly significant. The rescue operations are using a technique developed in Switzerland, called long line or short haul. And basically, what they're doing is, they're attaching a long line from the bottom of the helicopter, and they're bringing a technician in at the end of the line. And they fly in close to the mountain. And they're able to literally, pluck a climber off of a ridge—or even a mountain 70 face, in some cases.

You know, the skills that are required to operate these machines are quite significant and, you know, the margin for error is quite small. And that was evident in the accident that I describe in the beginning of my story.

SIEGEL: Well, Nick Heil, thanks for talking with us today.

HEIL: Thank you, Robert.

SIEGEL: Nick Heil is a contributing editor at Outside magazine. He also wrote the book "Dark Summit: The True Story of Everest's Most Controversial Season."

Close Read

What are the advantages of the Swiss rescue technique? Cite text evidence in your response.

_____

_____

1. Analyze   2. Practice   3. Perform

Source 2: Informational Article

Why Everest?

by Guy Moreau

In 1953, the New Zealander Edmund Hillary and the Sherpa Tenzing Norgay became the first people to reach the 29,035-foot peak of Mount Everest. Since that time, nearly 4,000 other people have successfully scaled the world's highest mountain. The youngest is an American boy who made the climb when he was 13 years old; the oldest is a Japanese woman who was 73 years old when she made her second successful climb.

Not everyone manages to complete the climb, and some
10 of these people pay with their lives. There have been over 230 deaths on the mountain.

Alan Arnette is a mountaineer who reached the summits of the tallest mountains on each of the seven continents in a single year. He has climbed Everest four times and thinks that perhaps 200 dead bodies remain on the mountain. The body of one climber who died in 1996 still lies next to the trail on the north side and is used as a landmark identified by the green boots he is still wearing.

It has been 50 years since Hillary and Norgay made their
20 historic climb, and the ascent is not as treacherous as it was. Sherpa guides know where they should put ropes and the paths the climbers should take. So why do so many people die in their attempts?

One thing to bear in mind is that climbers not only have to reach the summit safely, they also have to make their way back down. By that time, they are tired and may have run low on oxygen. They may have faced bad weather, and they have struggled up the icy slopes of the "death zone." This is the part of the climb above 26,247 feet, where the final camp before

30 the summit is located. A person cannot survive in this zone for more than two days because of the lack of oxygen and the extreme temperatures.

In recent years, this problem has been made worse by the large number of climbers who want to conquer Everest. The climbing season only lasts for about two months, if that, when the winds on the mountain are not as powerful as during the rest of the year. Climbers need to leave the final camp by late morning. Then, there can be so many of them in the death zone that there are traffic jams. Some days, up to 200 people set off.

40 Climbers are delayed and can suffer exposure and use their precious supplies of oxygen.

There is also another problem facing some climbers: they may not be skilled enough. Nobody doubts their strength and fitness, but they may not know enough about mountaineering and the hazards that high altitudes present. The paths have been prepared by hundreds of Sherpas and the hardships seem less than they would have been years ago. So people can get lulled into thinking that it isn't such an ordeal.

Given these difficulties, the months of preparation, and

50 the thousands of dollars paid for a permit, why do more and more people want to challenge the world's highest mountain? Well, it seems that the question includes the answer. It's because it is the world's highest mountain. It's the biggest feather in

Close Read

Why does climbing Everest have such a high fatality rate? Cite evidence from the text in your response.

_____

1. Analyze   2. Practice   3. Perform

a mountaineer's cap. Rhys Jones, and English climber who completed the ascent of Everest on his twentieth birthday, explained to the BBC: "Everyone is aware of the risks. . . . But actually, risk is part of the attraction—it makes it more of a test, it gives you more to aim for."

60   Rhys Jones probably has it right, but it's been said in fewer words. George Mallory, before his fatal attempt to scale Everest in 1924, explained why he wanted to climb the mountain: "Because it's there."

Close Read

Summarize the challenges faced by Everest's climbers. Cite textual evidence in your response.

_____

_____

_____

_____

Source 3: Newspaper Article

The Seattle Times

THURSDAY, JUNE 21, 2012

Ranger Killed During Rescue of Climbers on Mount Rainier

A ranger with Mount Rainier National Park died Thursday afternoon while rescuing climbers, two of whom had fallen into a crevasse.

Nick Hall, a climbing ranger at Mount Rainier National Park, fell 3,700 feet to his death Thursday afternoon, after helping rescue two climbers who had fallen into a crevasse, according to a park news release. The two women who fell into the crevasse were part of a party of four, two women and two men, from Waco, Texas.

10 As Hall, 34, was preparing some of the climbers for helicopter evacuation at 4:59 p.m., he fell down the mountain's northeast side from the 13,700-foot level. He was not moving after his fall, and attempts to contact him were unsuccessful, the release said.

Climbers reached him hours later and confirmed he had died.

Hall, a native of Patten, Maine, had been with the park's climbing program for four years, the release said.

The climbers who fell into the crevasse had slipped on their 20 descent down Emmons Glacier after hiking to Mount Rainier's 14,411-foot summit around 1:45 p.m. Thursday.

As the two women were dangling inside the crevasse at the 13,700-foot level, one of the other climbers was able contact rescue rangers by cellphone.

1. Analyze 2. Practice 3. Perform

The rescue team was able to reach the climbers fairly fast.

The two women climbers were pulled to safety by 3:10 p.m. The four climbers, who range in age from 18 to 53, have injuries from slipping and having a few hundred pounds of force yank on their harnesses at the end of the fall, but none are life-
30 threatening, said Kevin Bacher, a park spokesman.

A rapidly lowering cloud ceiling and 40-mph winds made it tough for a Chinook helicopter from Joint Base Lewis-McChord to reach the climbers, but three were eventually lifted away at around 9 p.m., Bacher said.

The fourth climber stayed on the mountain overnight with rescue rangers.

They started down Friday morning, but the park still hoped a helicopter would be able to pick her up and also recover Hall's body, Bacher said. Six rangers went to recover Hall's body, but
40 that could take several days if the helicopter can't fly.

The three climbers rescued were hospitalized and are in fair condition today.

Hall's family told The Associated Press that they were proud of him for his involvement in mountain rescues.

"We sincerely hope the loss of our son will draw appropriate attention to the hazards and safety requirements and commitment to be involved in the profession and sport he so loved," said his father, Carter Hall, from the family home in Patten, Maine.

50 The family said it was "grieving and celebrating" his life.

Close Read

What details in the article suggest that services should not be provided to people who put themselves at risk? Cite text evidence in your response.

_____

_____

Respond to Questions on Step 3 Sources

These questions will help you analyze the sources you've read. Use your notes and refer to the sources in order to answer the questions. Your answers to these questions will help you write your essay.

1 Is the evidence from one source more credible than the evidence from another source? When you evaluate the credibility of a source, examine the expertise of the author and/or the organization responsible for the information. Record your reasons.

Source	Credible?	Reasons
Radio Interview Helicopter Rescues Increasing on Everest		
Informational Article Why Everest?		
Newspaper Article Ranger killed during rescue of climbers on Mount Rainier		

2 **Prose Constructed-Response** What point about the rescue of mountain climbers is raised in all three sources? Why is this point important to address when making an informed decision about the demands of climbers to be rescued? Cite text evidence in your response.

_____

_____

_____

3 **Prose Constructed-Response** Does the information in the article "Ranger killed during rescue of climbers on Mount Rainier" support or contradict the argument found in the interview "Helicopter Rescues Increasing on Everest"? Cite text evidence in your response.

_____

_____

Part 2: Write

Plan

Use the graphic organizer to help you outline the structure of your argumentative essay.

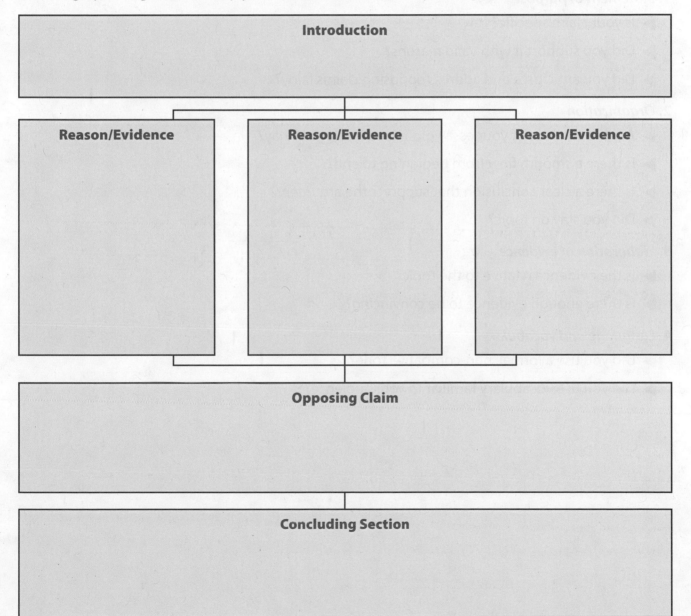

Introduction

Reason/Evidence   Reason/Evidence   Reason/Evidence

Opposing Claim

Concluding Section

Draft

 Use your notes and completed graphic organizer to write a first draft of your argumentative essay.

Revise and Edit

Look back over your essay and compare it to the Evaluation Criteria. Revise your essay and edit it to correct spelling, grammar, and punctuation errors.

Evaluation Criteria

Your teacher will be looking for:

1. *Statement of purpose*

▶ Is your claim specific?

▶ Did you support it with valid reasons?

▶ Did you anticipate and address opposing claims fairly?

2. *Organization*

▶ Are the sections of your essay organized in a logical way?

▶ Is there a smooth flow from beginning to end?

▶ Is there a clear conclusion that supports the argument?

▶ Did you stay on topic?

3. *Elaboration of evidence*

▶ Is the evidence relative to the topic?

▶ Is there enough evidence to be convincing?

4. *Language and vocabulary*

▶ Did you use a formal, non-combative tone?

▶ Did you use vocabulary familiar to your audience?

© Houghton Mifflin Harcourt Publishing Company

Things Change

Informational Essay

ANALYZE THE MODEL

Evaluate two informative essays about the universe and planets.

PRACTICE THE TASK

Write an informative essay about the presence of pythons in the everglades.

PERFORM THE TASK

Write an informative essay about scientific knowledge, its change over time, and its effect on society.

An informative essay, or expository essay, is a short nonfiction work that tells a reader facts about a topic. The purpose of a nonfiction piece is to convey information. Examples of nonfiction writing are newspaper articles, online articles, magazine articles, encyclopedia articles, and speeches.

The nonfiction topics that you will read about in this unit discuss factual changes in scientific knowledge. The information in these selections is factual.

IN THIS UNIT, you will analyze information from a variety of nonfiction articles from magazines and newspapers. You will find, organize, and present facts that will add to your readers' knowledge of a topic. Your success will depend on how well you select evidence to support your topic.

STEP 1
ANALYZE THE MODEL

Why does our knowledge of the universe change over time?

You will read:

▶ **AN INSTRUCTIONAL ESSAY**
Starting Strong

You will analyze:

▶ **TWO STUDENT MODELS**
A Universe of Knowledge

Planet X or Dwarf Planet?

Source Materials for Step 1

Ms. Rogers' students read the following text to help them learn strategies for writing informative essays. As you read, underline information that you find useful.

Starting Strong

Researching a fact or two usually isn't challenging. Researching a topic and planning and writing an informative essay, however, is a complex process. A successful informative essay conveys factual information from several sources and presents that information in a logical way that leads to an overall conclusion.

When you write an essay, the parts should *relate* to each other in a clear way to support your message. Graphic organizers like the basic framework for an informative report below, can help you plan your organizational structure.

Framework for an Informational Essay

Introduction
Hook your reader's interest and clearly identify your subject. Make your topic and main point clear.

Body
Discuss each main idea in one or more paragraphs and support each main idea with facts, examples, and quotations.

Conclusion
Bring your report to a close by tying your ideas together. Summarize or restate your main idea(s) or draw conclusions.

Main Idea and Supporting Details

The main ideas that you develop in the body of your informative essay will be supported by two or more details, descriptions, or explanations. The graphic organizer below will help you organize your ideas and the details you will use to explain them. Jot down a main idea or central point. Then identify the details you will use to support your main idea. To keep on track, refer regularly to your graphic organizer as you write.

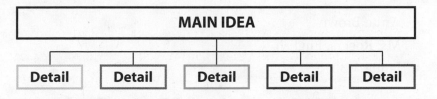

Narrative Description: Painting with Specifics

Informative essays often require descriptive language to help the reader understand the topic being discussed, especially if you want to describe specific people, events, or procedures. Narrative description is used to explain an event is usually organized chronologically, with details presented in time order. A graphic organizer such as the one below can help you incorporate narrative description into your informative essay. Facts, sensory details, and actions are three types of specifics you can include.

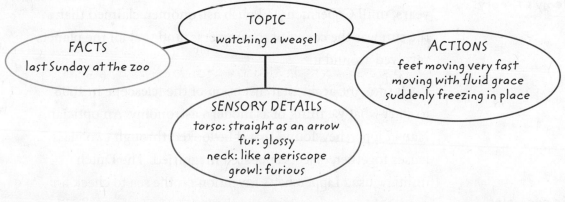

Discuss and Decide

Explain how you might use narrative description in an informative essay on Civil War drummer boys. What events would you describe? Think about duties, uniforms, and the boys themselves.

Analyze Two Student Models for Step 1

Anita developed her topic by supporting it with five main ideas that were each covered in a paragraph in the body of her essay. Read her essay closely. The red side notes are comments made by her teacher, Ms. Rogers.

Anita's Model

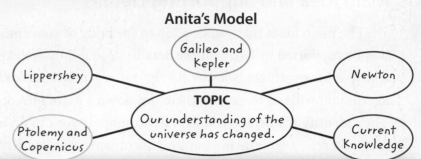

Galileo and Kepler

Lippershey

Newton

TOPIC Our understanding of the universe has changed.

Ptolemy and Copernicus

Current Knowledge

Anita Brown

Ms. Rogers, English

January 30

A Universe of Knowledge

What we understand about the universe has changed over history, and it will probably continue to change.

The first person to suggest that Earth revolved around the sun was the Greek astronomer Aristarchus of Samos, in the third century BC. Most people rejected his ideas later in favor of Ptolemy, who stated that Earth was the center of the universe, and that the sun, moon, and stars all revolved around it. Ptolemy's theories were taken as fact for about 1,400 years, until Copernicus, a Polish astronomer, claimed that the sun was the center of the universe, and that all the planets revolved around it.

It took the accidental invention of the telescope in 1608 to start what we think of as modern astronomy. An optician, Hans Lippershey, found that if he looked through two glass lenses together, objects appeared magnified. The Dutch military used Lippershey's invention on the sea to check for approaching enemy ships, but the Italian astronomer Galileo Galilei decided to use the telescope to look at the stars.

Mentioning the future is a good way to hook your readers!

Why didn't anyone believe him? Were people too connected to Ptolemy's theory?

Specific examples support your main idea. Each discovery had to build on one before.

1. Analyze   2. Practice   3. Perform

Galileo discovered that Jupiter had moons orbiting it, he saw that the Milky Way was actually made up of billions of individual stars, and he agreed with Copernicus's idea that the sun was the center of our solar system. But Galileo was found guilty of heresy and was put under house arrest for the rest of his life. In Germany, however, the work of Johannes Kepler supported Galileo's ideas. People began to accept that the planets move around the sun, but it would take over 40 years to understand why they move around the sun.

In England, Sir Isaac Newton had developed his own theory about why the planets move around the sun. He determined that the force of gravity that made an apple fall from a tree to the ground was the same force that held the planets in their orbits in space.

Inventions such as photography and the discoveries of various forms of light have pushed our knowledge of the universe further. In the twentieth century, astronomers learned that here are 100 billion stars in our galaxy, and there are hundreds of billions of galaxies. In this century, we have found out that there are probably 17 billion Earth-sized planets in our galaxy.

How will our knowledge of the universe change? We cannot tell, but the one thing we do know is that our ideas will change.

Technology has definitely advanced our understanding of the universe!

Discuss and Decide

How did Anita's main ideas relate to her topic? Cite textual evidence in your discussion.

Joseph used chronological order to develop the main ideas that support his topic. Ms. Rogers made her notes in red.

Joseph's Main Ideas About Pluto

| 1930 Orbits of Neptune and Uranus | → | 1978 Discovery of Charon | → | 1979 Pluto's unusual orbit | → | 1989 Orbits of Neptune and Uranus | → | 2006 Pluto's planet status |

Joseph Keegan
Ms. Rogers, English
January 30

Planet X or Dwarf Planet?
A Century in the Study of Pluto

Nice setup of your topic.

Over 100 years ago, the astronomer Percival Lowell started looking for Planet X, a planet he thought should exist beyond Neptune. His theory was that there had to be a planet whose gravitational pull affected the orbits of Neptune and Uranus.

It wasn't until 1930 that the mystery planet was found, very close to the point it was expected to be. Planet X was renamed Pluto, a name proposed by an 11-year-old girl from Oxford, England. The name pleased astronomers, as it began with Percival Lowell's initials.

Detail is supported with fact-based evidence.

In 1978, astronomers discovered Charon, one of Pluto's moons. This allowed them to calculate the mass of Pluto, and they discovered that Lowell's theory had been wrong—Pluto's gravitational pull on Neptune and Uranus was insignificant.

Although Pluto is the farthest planet, the next year an event occurred that takes place every 248 years. Because of Pluto's particular orbit, Neptune became the farthest planet from the sun. This lasted until 1999.

In 1989, *Voyager 2* allowed astronomers to calculate Neptune's mass more accurately, and they found that there really was no discrepancy in the orbits of Neptune and Uranus.

Good way to show how advancements in science have allowed us to get more accurate information.

In 2005, two more of Pluto's moons were discovered. The International Astronomical Union (IAU) named them Nix and Hydra. But later in 2006, the IAU made another announcement: Pluto is no longer considered a planet in our solar system. It is now classified as a "dwarf planet." The decision means that Neptune will now be considered the eighth and last planet in our solar system.

So, students will no longer remember the order of the planets by saying "My very eager mother just served us nine pizzas" (Mercury, Venus, Earth, Mars, Jupiter, Saturn, Uranus, Neptune, Pluto). We will have to think of another mnemonic.

Very true! Any suggestions?

Close Read

Why did it make sense for Anita and Joseph to present their essays in chronological order? Cite text evidence in your response.

_____

_____

_____

Terminology of Informative Essays

Read each term and explanation. Then look back and analyze each
student model. Find an example to complete the chart. Finally, make a
claim about which model was more successful in illustrating each term.

Term	Explanation	Example from Student Essays
topic	The **topic** is a word or phrase that tells what the essay is about.	
text structure	The **text structure** is the organizational pattern of an essay.	
focus	The **focus** is the controlling, or overarching, idea that states the main point the writer chooses to make.	
supporting evidence	The **supporting evidence** is relevant quotations and concrete details that support the focus.	
domain-specific vocabulary	**Domain-specific vocabulary** is content-specific words that are not generally used in conversation.	
text features	**Text features** are features that help organize the text, such as: headings, boldface type, italic type, bulleted or numbered lists, sidebars, and graphic aids, including charts, tables, timelines, illustrations, and photographs.	

Claim:_____

Support your claim by citing text evidence.

_____

_____

1. Analyze   2. Practice   3. Perform

How is the presence of Burmese pythons changing the Everglades?

You will read:

▶ **AN INFORMATIONAL ARTICLE**
Burmese Python: Not the Ideal Pet

▶ **A NEWSPAPER ARTICLE**
Florida's Python Hunt

▶ **AN ADVERTISEMENT**
Python Challenge

▶ **A BLOG**
Burmese Python: The Ecosystem Challenge

You will write:

▶ **AN INFORMATIVE ESSAY**
How is the presence of Burmese pythons changing the Everglades?

Source Materials for Step 2

AS YOU READ You will be writing an informative essay on the topic of Burmese pythons in Florida's Everglades. Carefully study the sources in Step 2. Annotate the texts by underlining and circling information and evidence that may be useful when you write your essay.

Source 1: Informational Article

Burmese Python: Not the Ideal Pet

by Matt Piven

The Burmese python is a magnificent and powerful animal. Native to the grassy marshes of Southeast Asia, it is among the largest snakes in the world, capable of growing to an astounding length of 23 feet and a weight of up to 200 pounds. Think of a telephone pole, and then imagine a snake as big around the middle as that pole. That's the Burmese python.

Burmese pythons are carnivores and survive primarily on small birds and mammals. Although they have no venom, they have other, quite effective means of killing their prey. Chemical receptors in their tongues and heat sensors along the jaws compensate for their poor eyesight and allow them to hunt in the dark. To kill their prey, they first grasp it with their back-curving teeth. When the animal tries to pull away, it only sinks further into the python's grip. Then, the python coils its long and powerful body around the animal, squeezes until the animal dies, and swallows the animal whole. The python's unique hinged jaws allow it to swallow an object five times as wide as its own head.

Many people have chosen these unusual reptiles as pets, most likely because of the snakes' beautifully patterned skin, their rapid growth rate, and their generally docile disposition. Unfortunately, many of these owners, upon discovering that they had more snake than they could handle, have resorted to the worst possible solution and released the snakes back into the wild.

Source 2: Newspaper Article

January 5, 2013

FLORIDA'S PYTHON HUNT

by Andrew Ng

A growing population of Burmese pythons—many pets turned loose by their owners when they became too big—is threatening the ecosystem of Florida's Everglades. With no natural predators, these eating machines appear to be wiping out huge numbers of opossums, raccoons, and bobcats, as well as many bird species.

Tens of thousands of Burmese pythons are estimated to be living in the Everglades, where they thrive in the warm, humid climate. In a dramatic demonstration intended to underscore the threat posed by these snakes, Florida Senator Bill Nelson actually took the skin from a 16-foot Burmese python to a Senate committee hearing on the subject.

To address the problem, the state's Fish and Wildlife Commission is sponsoring its first-ever Python Challenge. Open to the public from Jan. 12 until Feb. 10, the challenge is to hunt and kill Burmese pythons, with a grand prize of $1,500 awarded to the hunter who kills the most pythons, and another $1,000 to the hunter who bags the longest one. Prizes will be awarded in two divisions: one for novices and the other for those who already have python hunting permits.

This means that for 30 days, hundreds of people armed with shotguns, rifles, machetes, handguns, and hooked spears—many who have never even seen a Burmese python—will roam the Florida Everglades in search of the coveted snakes. Our advice: If you happen to be in the area, be sure to wear a bulletproof vest.

Discuss and Decide

Which seems the greater risk to Florida: the problem of too many Burmese pythons, or the solution in which untrained hunters are competing for cash prizes to hunt them? Cite text evidence to support your answer.

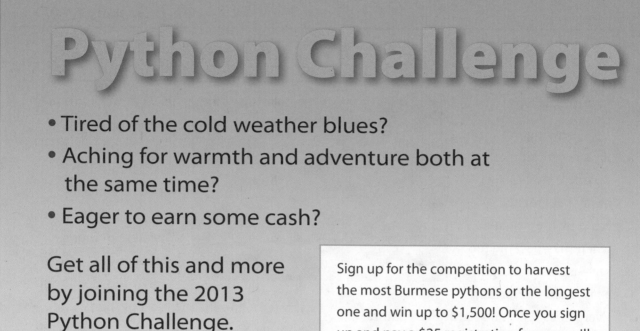

Python Challenge

- Tired of the cold weather blues?
- Aching for warmth and adventure both at the same time?
- Eager to earn some cash?

Get all of this and more by joining the 2013 Python Challenge.

Sign up for the competition to harvest the most Burmese pythons or the longest one and win up to $1,500! Once you sign up and pay a $25 registration fee, you will learn from experts how to identify, handle, and harvest these giant snakes. You'll also gain valuable information on the effect of this invasive species on the Florida everglades and its native wildlife.

Join the fun at PythonChallenge.org

The Florida Fish and Wildlife Conservation Commission, host of the Challenge, welcomes people from all parts of the country to participate.

Source 4: Blog

Burmese Python
The Ecosystem Challenge
by EcoEchoes

Enter your email address:

Subscribe by Email

SEARCH

- www.blogspot.com
- EcoEchoes
- About / FAQ
- Surprise me!

I'm not in love with the idea of the Python Challenge. Yes, the alarming growth of Burmese pythons in the Everglades is a big problem. And, yes, if we want to preserve the ecosystem of the Everglades, we have to address it. But is challenging people from all over the country to come down and kill some pythons really going to solve the problem?

I don't think so. It's not by accident that the Burmese python, a native of Southeast Asia, ended up in the Everglades. Their appearance in Florida is totally a man-made event, largely the result of the lucrative exotic pet market.

Some of the "proud" owners of Burmese pythons are—well, there's just no polite way to put this—just downright stupid. Can you imagine buying a wild animal without researching anything about it? And, when their pythons got too big, the owners got rid of them in the most irresponsible fashion: They just let them go into the Everglades or some other wild area. Hurricane Andrew didn't help matters. An exotic pet dealer's warehouse that housed nearly 900 Burmese pythons was destroyed, and many of its pythons escaped.

It's not enough to say, "Let's go out and shoot some pythons." These animals are in Florida because we brought them here. We must do a better job of educating people about the effect their careless actions have on ecosystems here in Florida and around the world.

Discuss and Decide

Explain the solution EcoEchoes advocates. Cite text evidence in your response.

Respond to Questions on Step 2 Sources

The following questions will help you think about the sources you've read. Use your notes and refer to the sources as you answer the questions. Your answers to will help you write your essay.

1 Why is Florida's Python Hunt important to the Everglades?

   a. The tourists will help the economy.

   b. Florida has outlawed alligator challenges.

   c. Burmese pythons are destroying local animal populations.

   d. Burmese pythons are injuring people in the area.

2 Which words best support your answer to Question 1?

   a. "... it is among the largest snakes in the world, capable of growing to an astounding length of 23 feet and a weight of up to 200 pounds." (Source 1)

   b. "With no natural predators, these eating machines appear to be wiping out huge numbers of opossums, raccoons, and bobcats as well as many bird species." (Source 2)

   c. "... gain valuable information on the effect of this invasive species on the Florida Everglades and its native wildlife." (Source 3)

   d. "Their appearance in Florida is totally a man-made event, largely the result of the lucrative exotic pet market." (Source 4)

3 Which of these is a reason why the python should be hunted?

   a. Pythons are negatively affecting the local ecosystem.

   b. Thousands of pythons are living in the Everglades.

   c. Large rewards are being offered to capture and kill pythons.

   d. People who brought them here as pets created the problem.

4 What is a disadvantage to Florida's Python Hunt?

    a. It will eliminate all of the Burmese pythons in the area.

    b. People might get hurt.

    c. It's too late to fix the damage caused by the pythons.

    d. Too many tourists will hurt the local community.

5 Which words best support your answer to Question 4?

    a. "The python's unique hinged jaws allow it to swallow an object five times as wide as its own head." (Source 1)

    b. ". . . many who have never even seen a Burmese python . . ." (Source 2)

    c. "Dying to get some cash into your pitifully small bank account?" (Source 3)

    d. "These animals are in the Florida because we brought them here." (Source 4)

6 **Prose Constructed-Response** What is one claim you can make about humans' involvement in the python problem? Cite text evidence from at least two of the sources.

_____

_____

_____

_____

7 **Prose Constructed-Response** How does the Python Challenge affect people outside of Florida? Cite text evidence in your response.

_____

_____

_____

_____

Planning and Prewriting

Review your notes and sources before you start writing. Then decide what key idea you want to express and collect text evidence to support it.

 You may prefer to do your planning on a computer.

Introduce Your Topic

State your topic clearly: _____

_____

_____

Develop Your Topic with Relevant Facts and Evidence

Main idea and details about Burmese pythons: _____

_____

_____

Main idea and details about the changes in local animals: _____

_____

_____

Main idea and details about the changes in people: _____

_____

_____

Main idea and details about the changes in ecosystems: _____

_____

_____

Find Evidence

For each type of detail, cite text evidence that supports your topic.

Detail	Evidence

Finalize Your Plan

Use your responses and notes from previous pages to create a detailed plan for your essay and fill in the chart below.

▶ "Hook" your audience with an interesting detail, question, or quotation.

▶ Clearly introduce your topic.

Introduction

▶ State each main idea.

▶ Include relevant facts, concrete details, and other evidence that support your main ideas.

Main idea and details about Burmese pythons

Main idea and details about changes in local animals

Main idea and details about changes in people

Main idea and details about changes in ecosystem

▶ End your essay by tying your ideas together in a concluding statement. You may want to include your own thoughts or opinions about your topic.

Conclusion

© Houghton Mifflin Harcourt Publishing Company

Draft Your Essay

As you write, think about:

▶ **Audience:** Your teacher

▶ **Purpose:** Demonstrate your understanding of the specific requirements of an informational essay

▶ **Style:** Use a formal and objective tone.

▶ **Transitions:** Use words and phrases such as *for example* or *because* to create cohesion, or flow.

Revise

Revision Checklist: Self Evaluation

Use the checklist below to guide your analysis.

 If you drafted your essay on the computer, you may wish to print it out so that you can more easily evaluate it.

Ask Yourself	Tips	Revision Strategies
1. Does the introduction present your topic clearly and grab the audience's attention?	Underline sentences in the introduction that engage the readers.	Add an interesting question, fact, or observation to get the reader's attention.
2. Are your details relevant, do you present evidence for them, and do they support your main idea?	Circle evidence.	Add textual evidence and descriptive details, if necessary.
3. Are appropriate and varied transitions used to clarify ideas?	Place a checkmark next to each transitional word or phrase.	Add transitional words or phrases where needed to clarify the relationships between ideas.
4. Does the concluding section follow and sum up the details, showing how they support the main ideas? Does it give the audience something to think about?	Double underline the summary of key points in the concluding section. Underline the insight offered to readers.	Add an overarching view of key points or a final observation about the significance of the main idea.

Revision Checklist: Peer Review

Exchange your essay with a classmate's, or read it aloud to your partner. As you read and comment on your classmate's essay, focus on how clearly the main idea is supported by details. Help each other identify parts of the drafts that need strengthening, reworking, or even a complete new approach.

What To Look For	Notes for My Partner
1. Does the introduction present your topic and grab the audience's attention?	
2. Are your details relevant, do you present evidence for them, and do they support your main ideas?	
3. Are appropriate and varied transitions used to clarify ideas?	
4. Does the concluding section follow and sum up the details, showing how they support the main ideas? Does it give the audience something to think about?	

Edit

Edit your essay to correct spelling, grammar, and punctuation errors.

Why does scientific knowledge change over time?

You will read:

▶ **A MAGAZINE ARTICLE**
The Half-Life of Facts

▶ **A NEWSPAPER ARTICLE**
The Food Pyramid and Why It Changed

▶ **AN INFORMATIONAL TEXT**
The Explosion in What We Know About Life Forms

You will write:

▶ **AN INFORMATIVE ESSAY**
Why does scientific knowledge change over time?

Part 1: Read Sources

Source 1: Magazine Article

The Half-Life of Facts

by Samuel Arbesman

AS YOU READ *Identify key ideas and textual evidence to use in your essay. For example, "change" is likely to be a topic in all three selections.*

NOTES

An interviewer asked mathematician and author Samuel Arbesman why he wrote the book The Half-Life of Facts, *in which he explains why facts are always changing. Here is Arbesman's response.*

I want to show people how knowledge changes. You have to be on guard, so you are not shocked when your children come home to tell you that dinosaurs have feathers. You have to look things up more often and recognize that most of the stuff you learned when you were younger is not at the cutting edge. We are coming a lot closer to a true understanding of the world; we know a lot more about the universe than we did even just a few decades ago. It is not the case that just because knowledge is constantly being overturned we do not know anything. But too
10 often, we fail to acknowledge change.

Some fields are starting to recognize this. Medicine, for example, has got really good at encouraging its practitioners to stay current. A lot of medical students are taught that everything they learn is going to be obsolete soon after they graduate. There is even a website called "up to date" that constantly updates medical textbooks. In that sense we could all stand to learn from medicine; we constantly have to make an effort to explore the world anew—even if that means

just looking at Wikipedia more often. And I am not just
20 talking about dinosaurs and outer space. You see this same
phenomenon with knowledge about nutrition or childcare—the
stuff that has to do with how we live our lives.

Scientists now believe that young *Tyrannosaurus rex* dinosaurs first evolved with a thin coat of feathers to stay warm.

This *Dilong paradoxus* dinosaur is a small-sized, evolutionary predecessor of *Tyrannosaurus rex*. Even though he never had wings or flew, his fossils prove that the Tyrannosaurs evolved with primitive feathers.

Discuss and Decide

1. How could the solution for medical textbooks be applied to other sources of knowledge?

2. What specific changes does Arbesman propose? Cite examples from the text.

The Food Pyramid
and Why It Changed

by William Neuman, *The New York Times*, May 27, 2011

NOTES

The Obama administration is about to ditch the food pyramid, that symbol of healthy eating for the last two decades. In its place officials are dishing up a simple, plate-shaped symbol, sliced into wedges for the basic food groups and half-filled with fruits and vegetables.

The circular plate, which will be unveiled Thursday, is meant to give consumers a fast, easily grasped reminder of the basics of a healthy diet. It consists of four colored sections, for fruits, vegetables, grains, and protein, according to several people who have been briefed on the change. Beside the plate is a smaller circle for dairy, suggesting a glass of low-fat milk or perhaps a yogurt cup.

The new nutritional graphic to replace the food pyramid

Few nutritionists will mourn the passing of the pyramid, which, while instantly recognized by millions of American school kids, parents and consumers, was derided by nutritionists as too confusing and deeply flawed because it did not distinguish clearly between healthy foods like whole grains

1. Analyze   2. Practice   3. Perform

and fish and less healthy choices like white bread and bacon. A version of the pyramid currently appearing on cereal boxes, frozen dinners and other foods has been so streamlined and
30 stripped of information that many people have no idea what it represents.

"It's going to be hard not to do better than the current pyramid, which basically conveys no useful information," said Walter C. Willett, chairman of the nutrition department at the Harvard School of Public Health.

Close Read

What was wrong with the food pyramid? Cite evidence from the text in your response.

_____

_____

_____

_____

_____

_____

_____

The Explosion in What We Know About Life Forms

by Alan Cochev

NOTES

For hundreds of years, people have wondered if we have encountered most of the living things on Earth or not. During the last three centuries, scientists have attempted to answer this question by classifying organisms to measure the number of species that are known. But recently, changes in the system of classification—called *taxonomy*— are making scientists believe that there are far more species on Earth than we ever suspected, most of them undiscovered.

Systems of taxonomy go back at least two thousand years.

10 The ancient Greek philosopher Aristotle classified all living things as either plants or animals and further described animals as being of three types: those that live on land, those that live in water, and those that live in the air. Plants and animals were called by their common names. One of the confusions that arose from this way of naming organisms is that scientists could not be sure whether two similar creatures that lived in different places were actually the same organism called by two different names. For example, the third largest rodent in North America, sometimes called a woodchuck, is

20 called by many other names—groundhog, marmot, grass rat, earth pig, and even whistle pig.

In the 18th century, the Swedish botanist Carl Linnaeus created a new, complex system of taxonomy based largely on the similar structures that organisms have. This system grouped organisms into large kingdoms (*e.g.*, plants and animals) and smaller and smaller groupings called phyla,

© Houghton Mifflin Harcourt Publishing Company • Image Credits: ©Vittorio Bruno/Shutterstock

1. Analyze   2. Practice   3. Perform

classes, orders, families, genera, and species. The genus and species of each type of organism were used to name the organism, which at last gave each organism a unique name—in
30   the case of the woodchuck, *Marmota monax*.

Since the Linnaean taxonomy was first conceived, there have been some changes in the system as scientists learned more about organisms. For example, various life forms have been moved into three new kingdoms: Fungi (including mushrooms), Monera (bacteria), and Protists (protozoans and most algae). Also, scientists have added ranks below species: *subspecies* for animals and *varieties* for plants. But for the most part, the system devised by Linnaeus is still in use.

However, the information used by scientists to classify
40   organisms changed greatly in the 20th century. Molecular biology has given scientists additional information as to how organisms are related. Organisms that have similarities in their DNA and RNA are understood by scientists to be more closely related than organisms that lack similarities. Also, scientists now believe that when a characteristic (such as feathers) shows up in only one group of organisms, those organisms must be related.

The 20th century also provided an explosion in the number of new species that were discovered. Many of these species live
50   in places that were previously unexplored, such as the floors of the world's oceans or the eyelids of humans. Many other species have been found in places where life was unexpected, such as in hot springs or the stomachs of humans. New information from all these discoveries has caused scientists to reevaluate modern taxonomy. Two groups of organisms—bacteria and archaeans— are now considered to be so different from other organisms that a new level of organization, called *domains*, has been created above kingdoms. The three domains are Archaea (including organisms that live near ocean vents and in hot springs),
60   Bacteria, and Eucaryota (all other organisms).

Discuss and Decide

Why has the taxonomy system of Linnaeus remained popular despite new discoveries about species?

One of the important outcomes of scientists' greater understanding of the diversity of life is the impact it may have on estimates for the number of species of living things. For example, scientists now understand that among smaller species, there tends to be greater diversity in the number of species. For example, the number of species of mammals on Earth is about 5,500, while the number of insect species is known to be at least one million. Some scientists believe that a spoonful of soil may contain as many as ten thousand different species of bacteria.

70 In addition, the discovery of thousands of new species every year provides scientists with better information to predict the number of species in a group based on the diversity in a higher level of taxonomy (genus, family, order, etc.). The method is like estimating the size of the base of a pyramid by measuring how much it widens at the top. One recent study reported by scientist Camilo Mora used this technique to estimate the number of species of living things—discovered and undiscovered—at 7.8 million. This number excludes bacteria and archaeans, about which too little is known to

80 make meaningful estimates. Since scientists have currently catalogued about 1.2 million species, this would mean that about 85% of species on Earth are still undiscovered! This estimate may need to be revised as more information becomes available, but so far the predictions made by this study have proven reliable.

With new and improving technologies shining additional light on the nature of life, we find that the more we learn, the more we continue to be surprised.

Close Read

1. To which domain would we assign extremophiles that can survive in steam, in acid, and in high radiation?

_____

2. To which kingdom would we assign bread mold and mushrooms?

_____

1. Analyze | 2. Practice | 3. Perform

Respond to Questions on Step 3 Sources

The following questions will help you think about the sources you've read. Use your notes and refer to the sources as you answer the questions. Your answers to will help you write your essay.

1 What could Carl Linnaeus *not* have used as a method of classification in his taxonomy system?

a. DNA

b. the habitats of organisms

c. structure of organisms

d. appearance of organisms

2 Which words best support your answer to Question 1?

a. "Molecular biology has given scientists additional information as to how organisms are related."

b. "In the 18th century, the Swedish botanist Carl Linnaeus created a new, complex system of taxonomy based largely on the similar structures that organisms have."

c. "The ancient Greek philosopher Aristotle classified all living things as either plants or animals and further described animals as being of three types . . ."

d. "Some scientists believe that a spoonful of soil may contain as many as ten thousand different species of bacteria."

3 Why might a parent be shocked to learn that a dinosaur has feathers?

a. because their child knows more than the parent

b. because the parent didn't think dinosaurs were covered at length in schools

c. because when the parent was in school, this knowledge wasn't available

d. because the child was never interested in dinosaurs before

4 Prose Constructed-Response Why is it helpful that the new nutritional graphic is shaped like a table setting? Cite textual evidence to support your answer.

_____

_____

_____

_____

_____

5 Prose Constructed-Response How has Linnaeus's taxonomy system changed over the centuries? Explain. Cite evidence from the text in your response.

_____

_____

_____

_____

_____

1. Analyze   2. Practice   3. Perform

Part 2: Write

Plan

Use the graphic organizer to help you outline the structure of your informative essay.

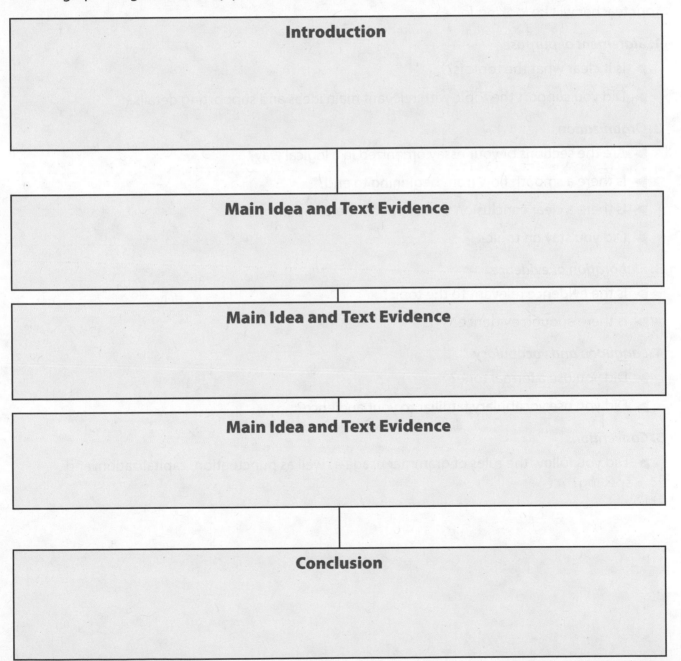

Introduction

Main Idea and Text Evidence

Main Idea and Text Evidence

Main Idea and Text Evidence

Conclusion

Draft

 Use your notes and completed graphic organizer to write a first draft of your essay.

Revise and Edit

Look back over your essay and compare it to the Evaluation Criteria. Revise your essay and edit it to correct spelling, grammar, and punctuation errors.

Evaluation Criteria

Your teacher will be looking for:

1. *Statement of purpose*

▶ Is it clear what the topic is?

▶ Did you support the topic with relevant main ideas and supporting details?

2. *Organization*

▶ Are the sections of your essay organized in a logical way?

▶ Is there a smooth flow from beginning to end?

▶ Is there a clear conclusion that supports the comparisons?

▶ Did you stay on topic?

3. *Elaboration of evidence*

▶ Is the evidence relevant to the topic?

▶ Is there enough evidence?

4. *Language and vocabulary*

▶ Did you use a formal tone?

▶ Did you use vocabulary familiar to your audience?

5. *Conventions*

▶ Did you follow the rules of grammar usage as well as punctuation, capitalization, and spelling?

Making Choices

Literary Analysis

© Houghton Mifflin Harcourt Publishing Company

STEP **1**	**ANALYZE THE MODEL**
	Analyze sound and symbol in the poem "Stopping by the Woods on a Snowy Evening" by Robert Frost.

STEP **2**	**PRACTICE THE TASK**
	Write an analysis of universal theme in "The Old Grandfather and His Little Grandson" and "Abuelito Who."

STEP **3**	**PERFORM THE TASK**
	Analyze characterization in Saki's "The Open Window."

Why do people love literature? Perhaps it's because literature shows us something important about life. Literature may not be based on facts, but what it reveals is truth. In addition, the way a work of literature is written reflects the author's choices and craft.

An author's choices begin with genre, or literary form. For example, is the literary work going to be a poem or a short story? What is the point of view going to be? Of course, the author's craft, including the use of specific word choice, figurative language, or irony, as well as structure, all make a literary work memorable and unique.

IN THIS UNIT, you will study a student's analysis of the poem "Stopping by Woods on a Snowy Evening" by Robert Frost. Then you will write a literary analysis comparing the folk tale "The Old Grandfather and His Little Grandson" by Leo Tolstoy with the poem "Abuelito Who" by Sandra Cisneros. Finally, you will analyze characterization in Saki's story "The Open Window."

STEP 1

▶ ANALYZE THE MODEL

How do I analyze a poem?

You will read:

▶ **A BIOGRAPHY**
Robert Frost: The Poet and His Craft

▶ **A POEM**
"Stopping by Woods on a Snowy Evening"

You will analyze:

▶ **A STUDENT MODEL**
Interpreting Sound and Symbol in Frost's "Stopping by Woods on a Snowy Evening"

Source Materials for Step 1

Mr. Miller assigned a poem by Robert Frost and a biography of the poet to his class to read and analyze. The notes in the side columns were written by Keisha Roberts, a student in Mr. Miller's class.

Robert Frost: The Poet and His Craft
by Lee Ann Windsor

I wonder why this place inspired him.

Winner of four Pulitzer Prizes, **Robert Frost** (1874–1963) was for many years our nation's best-known poet. Frost was born and raised in San Francisco until the age of eleven, when, after his father's death, he and his family moved to rural New England, the setting for nearly all his poetry. As a young man, Frost had tried raising chickens on a farm his grandfather had given him, but he was unsuccessful, for, as he once declared, "I'm not a farmer, that's no pose of mine."

Frost struggled to get his poems published. In 1912, he sought a complete change of scene by taking his family to England. The move turned out to be a wise one. There, he found a publisher for his first two collections of poems. The books became an instant success, and by the time he returned to the United States, he was a success on both sides of the Atlantic.

I should pay attention to his word choice and tone.

Known as the New England poet, Frost found his subjects in the landscapes and people of New England. In his poems, he used the everyday language and rhythms he heard in conversations with farmers. However, the plain speech and simple subjects of his poems, along with their imagery grounded in nature, disguise his poems' complex thoughts. Deceptively simple, Frost's poetry is filled with symbols, irony, and ambiguity. His rendering of the world is made complex by the layers of meaning embedded in his poems. Frost once said that poetry makes it possible to say one thing and mean another.

I'd better look for a deeper meaning in his poetry.

Discuss and Decide

Review the margin notes and the text. Then decide what characteristics you would look for in Frost's poetry. Cite textual evidence in your discussion.

1. Analyze   2. Practice   3. Perform

Stopping by Woods on a Snowy Evening
by Robert Frost

Whose woods these are I think I know.
His house is in the village, though;
He will not see me stopping here
To watch his woods fill up with snow.

5 My little horse must think it queer
To stop without a farmhouse near
Between the woods and frozen lake
The darkest evening of the year.

He gives his harness bells a shake
10 To ask if there is some mistake.
The only other sound's the sweep
Of easy wind and downy flake.

The woods are lovely, dark, and deep,
But I have promises to keep,
15 And miles to go before I sleep,
And miles to go before I sleep.

Who is the speaker? Why is he stopping here?

Why is he stopping when it is so dark?

The little horse "thinks"? He and the speaker communicate.

"Lovely" really contrasts with "dark and deep."

Why is the last line repeated?

Discuss and Decide

Reread the poem and review the margin notes. What addtional questions or comments do you have? Think of at least two.

Analyze a Student Model for Step 1

Read Keisha's literary analysis closely. The red side notes are comments from her teacher, Mr. Miller.

Keisha, this is a thoughtful analysis of a challenging poem.

Keisha Roberts,
Mr. Miller, English
December 6

Interpreting Sound and Symbol in Frost's
"Stopping by Woods on a Snowy Evening"

In Robert Frost's poem, "Stopping by Woods on a Snowy Evening," the speaker pauses to study a snowy woods on the "darkest evening of the year." The speaker is drawn to these "dark and deep" woods and does not wish to leave them. What is going on in this traveler's mind as he gazes at the woods?

Readers debate this poem's meaning. Some say that it is an appreciation of nature. Others say that it is about death. Some even argue that this poem is an early call by environmentalists against the disruption of civilization.

Important to bring in the different meanings of the poem.

In a literal interpretation, the speaker is tempted to stay because the woods are "lovely, dark, and deep," but he reminds himself of his "promises" and the miles still to go. Literally, snow is snow, a horse is a horse, and woods are woods. In Frost's hands, however, ordinary things become symbols. They stand for things other than themselves and suggest deeper layers of meaning.

The big question set up by the poem is what those lovely, dark, and deep woods symbolize to the traveler. They may symbolize a peaceful place free of stress and responsibilities, but ultimately he decides to pass them by.

Frost, who spoke often about the importance of the sound of a poem, wanted his readers to hear this poem as well as think about its meaning. "Stopping by Woods on a Snowy Evening" has a distinct rhythm and rhyme scheme. All but the last stanza has a rhyme scheme of AABA:

> Whose woods these are I think I know. **A**
> His house is in the village though; **A**
> He will not see me stopping here **B**
> To watch his woods fill up with snow. **A**

Frost uses a regular rhythm in this poem: "whose **woods** these **are** I **think** I **know**," which gives the poem a snappy pace that echoes the hoofbeats of the speaker's little horse, which the poet personifies. The language of this poem is very simple. In fact, most of the words in the poem have only one syllable. This simple word choice contributes to the rhythm of the poem.

Tell me more about the personification of the horse.

Even though the poem's words are simple, its message is deep. It is the mark of a great poem that its simple language and structure can have such meaning and depth for the reader. Frost's message that powerful desires pull people in one direction while daily responsibilities pull them in another has spoken to generations of readers.

Nice conclusion. I like the analysis of Frost's message and its relationship to his style. Well done, Keisha.

Discuss and Decide

Reread the poem and literary analysis. What would you add to this interpretation of the poem? Cite evidence from both texts in your discussion.

Terminology of Literary Analysis

Read each word and explanation. Then look back at Keisha Roberts's literary analysis and find examples to complete the chart.

Term	Explanation	Example from Keisha's Essay
speaker	In poetry, the **speaker** is the "voice" that talks to the reader, similar to the narrator in fiction. The speaker is not necessarily the poet.	
theme	The **theme** is the underlying message about life or human nature that the writer wants the reader to understand.	
symbol	A **symbol** is a person, a place, an object, or an activity that stands for something beyond itself.	
style	A **style** is a manner of writing. It involves *how* something is said rather than *what* is said.	
mood	**Mood** is the feeling or atmosphere that a writer creates for the reader through the use of imagery and descriptive words.	
rhythm	**Rhythm** is a pattern of stressed and unstressed syllables in a line of poetry. Poets use rhythm to emphasize ideas and create moods.	

How does an author develop a theme?

You will read:

▶ **AN INFORMATIVE ESSAY**
What Is a . . . Universal Theme

▶ **A FOLK TALE**
"The Old Grandfather and His Little Grandson"

▶ **A POEM**
"Abuelito Who"

You will write:

▶ **A LITERARY ANALYSIS**
What universal theme is expressed in the folk tale and the poem?

Source Materials for Step 2

AS YOU READ You will write an essay that compares the themes of the folk tale "The Old Grandfather and His Little Grandson" and the poem "Abuelito Who." Carefully read the following text about theme. As you read, underline and circle information that may be useful to you when you write your essay.

Source 1: Informative Essay

What Is a . . .

UNIVERSAL THEME
by Doris Sato

Universal Themes

No matter what we look like or where we come from, we are all made of the same stuff—we all have hearts and minds, feelings and thoughts. We all have hopes and fears, worries and dreams. We all experience both sorrows and joys. These universal concerns and experiences are the ties that bind us.

Writers translate these shared experiences into works of art that express universal themes. These themes are not restricted to literature from a particular time or place but appear over and over again. Writers, however, make these themes their own by adding their unique insights and perspectives and conveying themes in an original way.

Almost every culture has its folk tales, simple stories passed down for generations by word of mouth. Folk tales typically express a universal theme, a message about life or human nature that is so fundamental to human existence that it is true for all people of all time periods and cultures.

The Universal Language of Folk Tales

Folk tales began as an oral tradition and continue to be a vital part of many cultures today. Folk tales spread around the world as people moved from one place to another and blended with folk tales people heard in new locations. Interestingly, many cultures that have never interacted have folk tales with similar plots, motifs, and universal themes. This shows that no matter how different people are, they share basic experiences, concerns, and values.

Universal Themes Across Genres

Themes in literature tend to recur because human beings are more similar than different, no matter what the culture. The same themes often appear in different genres as well. Shakespeare expresses the theme of "the course of true love never runs smooth" in *Romeo and Juliet*, in *A Midsummer Night's Dream*, and in many of his sonnets. Yet a similar theme is also found in Roman mythology, poetry, and drama. You will find meaningful universal themes in literary works across genres and across centuries.

Folk heroes across centuries and cultures share characteristics such as strength and valor.

Discuss and Decide

Explain why folk tales often express universal themes. Cite specific evidence from the text.

Source 2: Folk Tale

The Old Grandfather and His Little Grandson
A Russian folk tale retold by Leo Tolstoy

The grandfather had become very old. His legs would not carry him, his eyes could not see, his ears could not hear, and he was toothless. When he ate, bits of food sometimes dropped out of his mouth. His son and his son's wife no longer allowed him to eat with them at the table. He had to eat his meals in the corner near the stove.

One day they gave him his food in a bowl. He tried to move the bowl closer; it fell to the floor and broke. His daughter-in-law scolded him. She told him that he spoiled everything in the house and broke their dishes, and she said that from now on he would get his food in a wooden dish. The old man sighed and said nothing.

A few days later, the old man's son and his wife were sitting in their hut, resting and watching their little boy playing on the floor. They saw him putting together something out of small pieces of wood. His father asked him, "What are you making, Misha?"

The little grandson said, "I'm making a wooden bucket. When you and Mamma get old, I'll feed you out of this wooden dish."

The young peasant and his wife looked at each other, and tears filled their eyes. They were ashamed because they had treated the old grandfather so meanly, and from that day they again let the old man eat with them at the table and took better care of him.

Discuss and Decide

Compare and contrast the behavior of the parents and the little grandson. What have the parents come to realize about themselves? Cite specific evidence from the text.

1. Analyze   2. Practice   3. Perform

Abuelito Who

by Sandra Cisneros

Abuelito° who throws coins like rain
and asks who loves him
who is dough and feathers
who is a watch and glass of water
5   whose hair is made of fur
is too sad to come downstairs today
who tells me in Spanish you are my diamond
who tells me in English you are my sky
whose little eyes are string
10   can't come out to play
sleeps in his little room all night and day
who used to laugh like the letter k
is sick
is a doorknob tied to a sour stick
15   is tired shut the door
doesn't live here anymore
is hiding underneath the bed
who talks to me inside my head
is blankets and spoons and big brown shoes
20   who snores up and down up and down up and down again
is the rain on the roof that falls like coins
asking who loves him
who loves him who?

---

1. **Abuelito:** Spanish for *granddaddy*

Close Read

Describe the relationship between the speaker and her grandfather. Cite
specific evidence from the text.

_____

_____

Respond to Questions on Step 2 Sources

These questions will help you analyze the sources you've read. Use your notes and refer to the sources in order to answer the questions. Your answers to these questions will help you write your essay.

1 Which of the following best summarizes a universal theme of both "The Old Grandfather and His Little Grandson" and "Abuelito Who"?

   a. Anyone may become old and sick.

   b. Grandchildren love and respect their grandparents.

   c. Older people use coins and wooden bowls.

   d. Children rarely understand older people.

2 In what ways is the treatment of the grandfather in the folk tale and the poem different?

   a. The grandfather in the folk tale is spoiled by the family.

   b. The grandfather in the poem is an active member of the family.

   c. The grandfather in the folk tale is treated badly.

   d. The grandfather in the poem is forced to move away.

3 Select the three pieces of evidence from the folk tale "The Old Grandfather and His Little Grandson" and from the speaker's observations in the poem "Abuelito Who" that best support your answer to Question 3.

   a. "His son and his son's wife no longer allowed him to eat with them at the table." ("The Old Grandfather and His Little Grandson," lines 4–5)

   b. His daughter-in-law scolded him. She told him that he spoiled everything . . ." ("The Old Grandfather and His Little Grandson," lines 8–9)

   c. "The old man sighed and said nothing." (line 11)

   d. "who tells me in Spanish you are my diamond / who tells me in English you are my sky . . . " (lines 7–8)

   e. "who used to laugh like the letter k . . . " ("Abuelito Who," line 12)

   f. "asking who loves him / who loves him who?" ("Abuelito Who," lines 22–23)

4 Prose Constructed-Response In "Abuelito Who," explain the speaker's feelings for her grandfather. How do you think the speaker would answer the question asked in lines 22–23 of the poem? Cite textual evidence in your response.

_____

_____

_____

_____

5 Prose Constructed-Response What characteristics do the grandfather and Abuelito share? Cite specific evidence from the folk tale and the poem.

_____

_____

_____

_____

6 Prose Constructed-Response What conclusion can you draw about the difference between the way the grandfather and Abuelito are regarded by their families? Cite textual evidence in your response.

_____

_____

_____

_____

Planning and Prewriting

Before you start writing, review your sources and determine the main points and supporting details to include in your essay. As you evaluate each point, collect textual evidence in the chart below.

 You may prefer to do your planning on a computer.

Decide on Key Points

Point	"The Old Grandfather . . ."	"Abuelito Who"
1. Characters ☑ Alike ☐ Different	Is elderly and sick	Is elderly and sick
2. Theme ☐ Alike ☐ Different		
3. Genre ☐ Alike ☐ Different		
4. Change in characters ☐ Alike ☐ Different		
5. Events/(plot/story) ☐ Alike ☐ Different		
6. Message expressed by theme ☐ Alike ☐ Different		

Identify the Text Structure

Before you write your essay, decide how you want to organize it. For both organizational strategies, your essay will begin with an introductory paragraph and end with a concluding paragraph.

Point-by-Point Discuss the first point of comparison or contrast for the folk tale "The Old Grandfather and His Little Grandson" and the poem "Abuelito Who." Then move on to the second point. If you choose this organization, you will read across the rows of this chart.

Topic	"The Old Grandfather . . ."	"Abuelito Who"	
1. Characters		→	If you use this organizational structure, your essay will have a paragraph comparing or contrasting the characters, followed by paragraphs comparing and contrasting the other topics in your chart.
2. Theme		→	
3. Genre		→	
4. Change in characters		→	
5. Mood		→	
6. Message expressed by theme		→	

Subject-by-Subject Discuss all the points about "The Old Grandfather and His Little Grandson" before moving on to "Abuelito Who." If you choose this method, you will be reading across the rows of this chart.

Selection	Characters	Theme	Genre	Change in characters	Mood	Message expressed by theme
1. "The Old Grandfather . . ."						→
2. "Abuelito Who"						→
If you use this organizational structure, your essay will have one or two paragraphs addressing all your points as they relate to "The Old Grandfather and His Little Grandson," followed by one or two paragraphs addressing all your points as they relate to "Abuelito Who."						

Finalize Your Plan

Use your responses and notes from previous pages to create a detailed plan for your essay.

▶ Hook your audience with an interesting detail, question, quotation, or anecdote.

▶ Identify what you will be comparing and contrasting, and state your controlling idea.

Introduction

▶ Follow a framework like the one shown here to organize your main ideas and supporting evidence.

▶ Include relevant facts, concrete details, and other text evidence. Restate your ideas.

Main Idea and Details

Main Idea and Details

Main Idea and Details

▶ Summarize the key points and restate your controlling idea.

▶ Include an insight that follows from and supports your controlling idea.

Conclusion

Draft Your Essay

As you write, think about:

▶ **Audience:** Your teacher

▶ **Purpose:** Demonstrate your understanding of the requirements of writing a literary analysis.

▶ **Style:** Use a formal and objective tone.

▶ **Transitions:** Use words and phrases such as *also, like, both,* and *in the same way* to show similarities, and *but, unlike,* and *by contrast* to show differences.

Revise

Revision Checklist: Self Evaluation

Use the checklist below to guide your analysis.

 If you drafted your essay on the computer, you may wish to print it out so that you can more easily evaluate it.

Ask Yourself	Tips	Revision Strategies
1. Does the introduction grab the audience's attention and include a controlling idea?	Draw a line under the attention-getting text. Circle the controlling idea.	Add an attention-getting sentence or idea. Make your controlling idea clear and exact.
2. Is each point of comparison supported by textual evidence, facts, and concrete details?	Circle textual evidence.	Add textual evidence, if necessary.
3. Are appropriate and varied transitions used to connect, compare, and contrast ideas?	Place a checkmark next to each transitional word or phrase.	Add words, phrases, or clauses to connect related ideas that lack transitions.
4. Does the concluding section restate the thesis statement and summarize ideas? Does it leave the audience with something to think about?	Double underline the summary of key points in the concluding section. Underline the insight offered to readers.	Add an overarching view of key points or a final observation about the significance of the comparison and contrast.

Revision Checklist: Peer Review

Exchange your essay with a classmate, or read it aloud to your partner. As you read and comment on your classmate's essay, focus on the statement of a universal theme and supporting textual evidence. Help each other identify parts of the draft that need strengthening, reworking, or a new approach.

What To Look For	Notes for My Partner
1. Does the introduction grab the audience's attention and include a controlling idea?	
2. Are there examples of ways in which the themes of the folk tale and the poem are alike, and ways in which they are different? Are the comparisons and contrasts supported by evidence from the texts?	
3. Are appropriate and varied transitions used to connect, compare, and contrast ideas?	
4. Does the concluding section restate the controlling idea and summarize ideas? Does it give the reader something to think about?	

Edit

Edit your essay to correct spelling, grammar, and punctuation errors.

1. Analyze   2. Practice   3. Perform

What techniques do authors use to create characters?

You will read:

▶ **AN INFORMATIVE ESSAY**
Characters: The Human Experience

▶ **A SHORT STORY**
"The Open Window"

You will write:

▶ **A LITERARY ANALYSIS**
How does Saki develop the characters of Nuttel and Vera in "The Open Window"?

Characters: The Human Experience

by John Leggett

© Houghton Mifflin Harcourt Publishing Company • Image Credits: Ken Usami/Photodisc/Getty Images

AS YOU READ *Pay close attention to the details explaining how authors develop characters. Record comments or questions about the text in the side margins.*

NOTES

Most of us are fascinated by other people. We like to know how other people deal with problems, disappointments, and temptations. A good story, whether it's true, made up, or somewhere in between, reveals some truth about human experience. It does this through the people who live on its pages—its characters.

Characterization: The Breath of Life

The way a writer reveals character is called characterization. Poor characterization can make even a real person uninteresting. Good characterization can make readers feel that 10 even fantasy characters—a bumbling teddy bear or a girl who is tossed by a tornado into an emerald city—live and breathe.

Creating Characters

A writer may simply tell us directly that a character is mean tempered or thrifty or brave or honest. This kind of characterization, called direct characterization, was often used by writers years ago. Present-day writers generally prefer to show their characters in action and let us decide for ourselves what kinds of people we are meeting. This method is called indirect characterization.

Direct Characterization

- Stating directly what a character is like.
20 Sergeant Randolph was the cruelest drillmaster in
  the regiment.

Indirect Characterization

- Describing the appearance of the character.
  Heather's hair was blood red, and every blood-red
  hair stuck up from her head. Underneath all that
  deep red hair, though, was a pair of baby blue
  eyes.
- Showing the character in action.
  Tony looked around, then tossed the empty soda
  can on the grass and kept going.
30
- Allowing us to hear the character speak.
  "I don't have to do what you say," declared Mina,
  pinching the new baby sitter.
- Revealing the character's thought and feelings.
  Donny didn't like the looks of the squash pudding
  but decided to eat some to please the cook.
- Showing how characters react to the character.
  "Go wake up my brother?" Lulu said. "Sure, Mom.
  Just give me a suit of armor and a twenty-foot
  pole, and I'll be good to go."

Motivation: How Could You Do That?

40   Why did your best friend suddenly get a crush on the
nerdiest guy in school? What could have possessed your brother
to think that he could complete that insane exercise routine?

We always wonder about people's motivation–that is, we
wonder what makes people behave the way we do. In real life we
may never learn the answer. Literature is different. In literature,
you'll find plenty of clues to characters' motives—why they do
the things they do. One of the pleasures of reading literature is
using these clues to figure out what makes people tick.

Discuss and Decide

Which type of character do you usually encounter in the stories you read: a
character developed by direct characterization or by indirect characterization?
Cite text evidence in your discussion.

The Open Window

by Saki (H. H. Munro)

AS YOU READ *Focus on the characters' words and actions. Record comments or questions about the text in the side margins.*

NOTES

"My aunt will be down presently, Mr. Nuttel," said a very self-possessed young lady of fifteen; "in the meantime you must try and put up with me."

Framton Nuttel endeavoured to say the correct something which should duly flatter the niece of the moment without unduly discounting the aunt that was to come. Privately he doubted more than ever whether these formal visits on a succession of total strangers would do much towards helping the nerve cure which he was supposed to be undergoing.

10 "I know how it will be," his sister had said when he was preparing to migrate to this rural retreat; "you will bury yourself down there and not speak to a living soul, and your nerves will be worse than ever from moping. I shall just give you letters of introduction to all the people I know there. Some of them, as far as I can remember, were quite nice."

Framton wondered whether Mrs. Sappleton, the lady to whom he was presenting one of the letters of introduction, came into the nice division.

"Do you know many of the people round here?" asked 20 the niece, when she judged that they had had sufficient silent communion.

Discuss and Decide

With a small group, discuss what you've learned about Framton Nuttel so far. What clue might his last name give to his personality? Cite text evidence in your response.

1. Analyze   2. Practice   3. Perform

"Hardly a soul," said Framton. "My sister was staying here, at the rectory, you know, some four years ago, and she gave me letters of introduction to some of the people here."

He made the last statement in a tone of distinct regret.

"Then you know practically nothing about my aunt?" pursued the self-possessed young lady.

"Only her name and address," admitted the caller. He was wondering whether Mrs. Sappleton was in the married

30   or widowed state. An undefinable something about the room seemed to suggest masculine habitation.

"Her great tragedy happened just three years ago," said the child;" that would be since your sister's time."

"Her tragedy?" asked Framton; somehow in this restful country spot tragedies seemed out of place.

"You may wonder why we keep that window wide open on an October afternoon," said the niece, indicating a large French window that opened on to a lawn.

"It is quite warm for the time of the year," said Framton;

40   "but has that window got anything to do with the tragedy?"

"Out through that window, three years ago to a day, her husband and her two young brothers went off for their day's shooting. They never came back. In crossing the moor to their favourite snipe-shooting ground they were all three engulfed in a treacherous piece of bog. It had been that dreadful wet summer, you know, and places that were safe in other years gave way suddenly without warning. Their bodies were never recovered. That was the dreadful part of it." Here the child's voice lost its self-possessed note and became falteringly human.

50   "Poor aunt always thinks that they will come back some day, they and the little brown spaniel that was lost with them, and walk in at that window just as they used to do. That is why

Close Read

What can you infer from the niece's earnest questioning? Why might it be significant that Nuttel is unfamiliar with the family?

_____

_____

the window is kept open every evening till it is quite dusk. Poor dear aunt, she has often told me how they went out, her husband with his white waterproof coat over his arm, and Ronnie, her youngest brother, singing 'Bertie, why do you bound?' as he always did to tease her, because she said it got on her nerves. Do you know, sometimes on still, quiet evenings like this, I almost get a creepy feeling that they will all walk in

60 through that window—"

She broke off with a little shudder. It was a relief to Framton when the aunt bustled into the room with a whirl of apologies for being late in making her appearance.

"I hope Vera has been amusing you?" she said.

"She has been very interesting," said Framton.

"I hope you don't mind the open window," said Mrs. Sappleton briskly; "my husband and brothers will be home directly from shooting, and they always come in this way. They've been out for snipe in the marshes to-day, so they'll

70 make a fine mess over my poor carpets. So like you men-folk, isn't it?"

She rattled on cheerfully about the shooting and the scarcity of birds, and the prospects for duck in the winter. To Framton it was all purely horrible. He made a desperate but only partially successful effort to turn the talk on to a less ghastly topic; he was conscious that his hostess was giving him only a fragment of her attention, and her eyes were constantly straying past him to the open window and the lawn beyond. It was certainly an unfortunate coincidence that he should have

80 paid his visit on this tragic anniversary.

"The doctors agree in ordering me complete rest, an absence of mental excitement, and avoidance of anything in the nature of violent physical exercise," announced Framton, who laboured under the tolerably wide-spread delusion that total strangers and chance acquaintances are hungry for the least detail of one's ailments and infirmities, their cause and cure. "On the matter of diet they are not so much in agreement," he continued.

"No?" said Mrs. Sappleton, in a voice which only replaced

90 a yawn at the last moment. Then she suddenly brightened into

alert attention—but not to what Framton was saying.

"Here they are at last!" she cried. "Just in time for tea, and don't they look as if they were muddy up to the eyes!"

Framton shivered slightly and turned towards the niece with a look intended to convey sympathetic comprehension. The child was staring out through the open window with dazed horror in her eyes. In a chill shock of nameless fear Framton swung round in his seat and looked in the same direction.

100 In the deepening twilight three figures were walking across the lawn towards the window; they all carried guns under their arms, and one of them was additionally burdened with a white coat hung over his shoulders. A tired brown spaniel kept close at their heels. Noiselessly they neared the house, and then a hoarse young voice chanted out of the dusk: "I said, Bertie, why do you bound?"

Framton grabbed wildly at his stick and hat; the hall-door, the gravel-drive, and the front gate were dimly noted stages in his headlong retreat. A cyclist coming along the road had to run into the hedge to avoid imminent collision.

110 "Here we are, my dear," said the bearer of the white mackintosh, coming in through the window; "fairly muddy, but most of it's dry. Who was that who bolted out as we came up?"

"A most extraordinary man, a Mr. Nuttel," said Mrs. Sappleton; "could only talk about his illnesses, and dashed off without a word of good-bye or apology when you arrived. One would think he had seen a ghost."

"I expect it was the spaniel," said the niece calmly; "he told me he had a horror of dogs. He was once hunted into a cemetery somewhere on the banks of the Ganges by a pack of 120 pariah dogs, and had to spend the night in a newly dug grave with the creatures snarling and grinning and foaming just above him. Enough to make anyone lose their nerve."

Romance at short notice was her speciality.

Discuss and Decide

With a small group, discuss what word other than *romance* you could use to describe Vera's activities. Why do you think the narrator chose this word? Cite evidence from the text in your discussion.

Respond to Questions on Step 3 Sources

These questions will help you think about the sources you have read. Use your notes and refer to the texts in order to answer the questions. Your answers will help you write your essay.

1 **Prose Constructed-Response** What aspects of Nuttel's personality might lead him to accept Vera's story? Cite specific evidence from the story.

_____

_____

_____

_____

2 **Prose Constructed-Response** What does Vera make Framton believe about her aunt? What does Vera explain to her aunt about Framton? What motivation could she have for these stories? Cite specific textual evidence.

_____

_____

_____

_____

3 **Prose Constructed-Response** *Vera* is a Latin word meaning "truth." How might Saki's choice of this name be an example of verbal irony (a contrast between what is said and what is actually meant)? Cite textual evidence in your response.

_____

_____

_____

_____

Part 2: Write

ASSIGNMENT

Write a literary analysis that answers the question: How does Saki develop the characters of Nuttel and Vera in "The Open Window"?

Plan

Use the graphic organizer to help you outline the structure of your literary analysis.

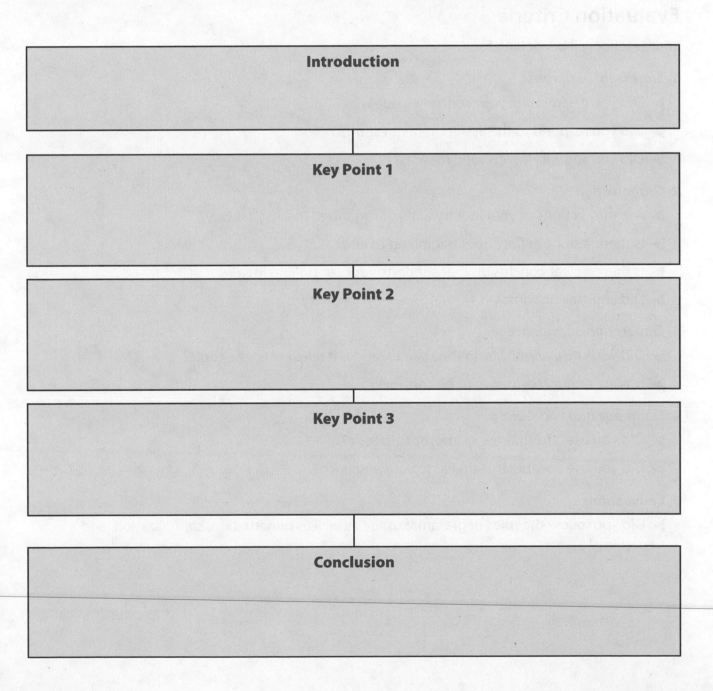

Introduction

Key Point 1

Key Point 2

Key Point 3

Conclusion

Draft

 Use your notes and completed graphic organizer to write a first draft of your literary analysis.

Revise and Edit

 Look back over your essay and compare it to the Evaluation Criteria. Revise your literary analysis and edit it to correct spelling, grammar, and punctuation errors.

Evaluation Criteria

Your teacher will be looking for:

1. Statement of purpose

▶ Did you clearly state your controlling idea?

▶ Did you respond to the assignment question?

▶ Did you support it with valid reasons?

2. Organization

▶ Are the sections of your literary analysis organized in a logical way?

▶ Is there a smooth flow from beginning to end?

▶ Is there a clear conclusion that supports your controlling idea?

▶ Did you stay on topic?

3. Elaboration of evidence

▶ Did you cite evidence from the sources, and is it relevant to the topic?

▶ Is there enough evidence to be convincing?

4. Language and vocabulary

▶ Did you use a formal, essay-appropriate tone?

▶ Did you use vocabulary familiar to your audience?

5. Conventions

▶ Did you follow the rules of grammar usage as well as punctuation, capitalization, and spelling?

On Your Own

RESEARCH SIMULATION

TASK 1 *Argumentative Essay*

RESEARCH SIMULATION

TASK 2 *Informative Essay*

TASK 3 *Literary Analysis*

RESEARCH SIMULATION

Argumentative Essay

Your social studies class is working on a special unit that's all about economic issues. Your teacher has assigned an argumentative essay about labor strikes.

First you will review three articles on labor strikes. After you have reviewed these sources, you will answer some questions about them. You should first skim the sources and the questions and then go back and read them carefully.

In Part 2, you will write an argumentative essay about whether you agree or disagree that public service workers should have the right to strike.

Time Management: Argumentative Task

There are two parts to most formal writing tests. Both parts of the tests are timed, so it's important to use your limited time wisely.

Part 1: Read Sources and Answer Questions

Preview the Assignment

35 minutes

You will have 35 minutes to read three sources and decide whether public service workers should have the right to strike. You will also answer questions that will help you plan your essay on the topic.

35 minutes! That's not much time.

Preview the questions. This will help you know which information you'll need to find as you read.

How Many?

How many pages of reading?

How many multiple-choice questions?

How many prose constructed-response questions?

How do you plan to use the 35 minutes?

Underline, circle, and take notes as you read. You probably won't have time to reread.

This is a lot to do in a short time.

Estimated time to read:

Source #1: "What Is a Strike?" [____] minutes

Source #2: "New York School Bus Strike" [____] minutes

Source #3: "Why Is It Rare for Public Sector Workers to Go on Strike?" [____] minutes

Estimated time to answer questions? [____] minutes

Total　　　　　　　　**35　minutes**

Any concerns?

_____

_____

Part 2: Write the Essay

70

How much time do you have? Pay attention to the clock!

Plan and Write an Argumentative Essay

70 minutes

You will have 70 minutes to plan, write, revise, and edit your essay.

Your Plan

Before you start to write, decide on your precise claim and reasons. Then think about the evidence you will use to support your reasons.

How do you plan to use the 70 minutes?

Estimated time for planning the essay?		minutes
Estimated time for writing?		minutes
Estimated time for editing?		minutes
Estimated time for checking spelling, grammar, and punctuation?		minutes
Total	**70**	**minutes**

Be sure to leave enough time for this step.

Notes:

_____

_____

_____

_____

Reread your essay, making sure that the points are clear. Check that there are no spelling or punctuation mistakes.

► Your Task

Your social studies class is working on a special unit that's all about economic issues. Your teacher has assigned an argumentative essay about strikes by public service workers—those workers who are employed by government agencies. In researching the topic, you have identified three sources you will use in planning your argumentative essay.

After you have reviewed the sources, you will answer some questions about them. Briefly skim the sources and the three questions that follow. Then, go back and read the sources carefully so you will have the information you will need to answer the questions. Take notes on the sources as you read. You may refer back to your notes at any time during Part 1 or Part 2 of the performance task.

► Part 1 (35 minutes)

You will now read the sources. After carefully reading the sources, use the rest of the time in Part 1 to answer the three questions about them. Though your answers to these questions will help you think about what you have read and plan your essay, they will also be scored as part of the test.

© Houghton Mifflin Harcourt Publishing Company

SOURCE #1:
What Is a Strike?

by Sharon Blumenstein

- A strike occurs when workers refuse to work until their working conditions have improved. Members of a workforce vote on whether or not they will strike. They can strike over a variety of issues: salary, benefits, unsafe working conditions, unpaid overtime, etc. Workers will strike if they cannot come to an agreement with their employer or change their employers' policies by using other means.

- Strikes are usually the most effective way that workers can use their strength as a group to improve their working
10   conditions.

- With the exception of federal government workers, those employed in the U.S. have a legal right to strike.

- Even if workers strike, there is no guarantee that the employer will meet their demands. Workers are not paid during a strike. Furthermore, workers participating in a strike run the risk of losing their jobs if their employer decides to hire replacement workers.

NOTES

Am I on Track?

Actual Time Spent Reading

SOURCE #2:
New York School Bus Strike: Sign of National Pressure on Unions

While New York City is seeking to bring down its highest-in-the-nation school busing costs by putting the contract out to bid, the union is demanding that drivers and matrons be protected.

by Stacy Teicher Khadaroo, staff writer

Christian Science Monitor

January 18, 2013

The New York City school bus strike is now in its third day—pitting the union's concerns over job security and bus safety against the city's need to bring down bus costs that are the highest in the nation.

It's also another indication—along with the recent teacher strike in Chicago and the fights over union rights in Wisconsin and elsewhere—that unions nationwide are increasingly feeling "their backs are to the wall," says Ed Ott, a distinguished lecturer in labor studies at the City University of New York's
10 Murphy Institute and the former head of the New York City Labor Council.

"Strikes were always considered the ultimate weapon, and you don't use them lightly," he says. "For this generation of union leaders, [the use of strikes] is a clear indication of the pressures they are feeling."

About 152,000 students—11 percent of public school students in New York—rely on school buses, which cover 7,700 routes. Forty percent of the buses were running Wednesday, the city said, because they are not driven by members of the
20 striking Amalgamated Transit Union Local 1181.

Other bused students have had to find alternative ways to school since Wednesday. The city has been providing metro cards and reimbursing families for driving or sending students in taxis, but that hasn't quelled the frustrations of some parents who have had their work schedules disrupted. Some parents, on the other hand, support the strikers.

The nationwide attention that strikes, rooted in very local fights, tend to receive now is another indication of how unions have weakened in recent decades. "It's sad that it's
30 seen as a novelty," says Zev Eigen, associate professor of law at Northwestern University. It also means that unions have to pick their fights carefully, he says, because public sympathy will go down if a strike is not tied to a substantial issue of fairness.

Am I on Track?

Actual Time Spent Reading

Why Is It Rare for Public Sector Workers to Go on Strike?

by Mia Lewis

Strikes by public sector workers (teachers, trash collectors, firefighters, and the like) do not happen often. Is it because these workers have high salaries, plum working conditions, and generous benefits, and therefore nothing to complain about? Or are there particular reasons why strikes in the public sector are especially rare?

First of all, it is important to remember that while workers in the private sector have a legally protected right to strike (with the exception of a few job categories), those who are employed

10 by the federal government do not. That means you won't see picket lines in the national parks, at the post office, or at the social security office.

State and city employees can only strike if there are state statutes that specifically allow them to—even then, some types of workers such as police and firefighters are permanently exempted and can never strike. While this may seem unfair, let's consider why the policy is in place. If workers in a widget factory strike for higher wages, their actions can't directly hurt anyone except themselves and their employers. However, the

20 general public would be in danger if police and firefighters did not report to work.

This is what happened during a police union strike in Boston in 1919. Criminals went on a rampage after police refused to work. Public opinion on the strike was very negative. The incident was a big setback for unions and labor in general.

Today, public sector strikes are very rare even when they are legal. Take strikes by teachers, for example. A teachers' strike in Chicago in September of 2012 was the first in the city in 25 years. With difficult working conditions and not overly

30 generous pay and benefits, one might expect the teachers' union

© Houghton Mifflin Harcourt Publishing Company

about politics and public opinion. Public sector employees serve the public, and so the public has an interest in seeing the strike come to an end. To win the strike, the teachers not only have to come out with a better contract, but they also have to be seen as righteous and worthy by the public.

Even if parents support teachers, they are unlikely to be sympathetic when they walk off the job and leave the kids— and parents—in a difficult situation. Even if the strike is over 40 better teacher-student ratios and other changes that will benefit students, it is difficult for teachers to maintain public support once they are on strike.

Instead of striking, most public sector unions solve disputes with their employers through mediation or arbitration. Mediation takes place when an impartial party oversees the negotiation to resolve differences. Arbitration occurs when an independent outsider looks at evidence submitted by both sides and comes up with a solution that is binding for all. If a fair contract can be reached, it is certainly better for all parties 50 involved, including the public.

Am I on Track?

Actual Time Spent Reading

Part 1 Questions

Answer the following questions. You may refer to your reading notes, and you should cite text evidence in your responses. Your answers to these questions will be scored. You will be able to refer to your answers as you write your essay in Part 2.

1 According to Source #1, which of the following best states the importance of workers' right to strike?

   a. Workers cannot get paid overtime unless they strike.

   b. Striking yields better results than agreeing to a new contract does.

   c. Federal government employees have demonstrated the power of the right to strike.

   d. Striking is usually the most effective way for a group of workers to improve their working conditions.

2 **Prose Constructed-Response** In Source #2, Ed Ott says that unions feel "their backs are to the wall." What details in this source support this statement? Include evidence from Source #3 in your response.

_____

_____

_____

_____

3 **Prose Constructed-Response** Why is going on strike a risky decision for public service employees?

_____

_____

_____

_____

_____

▶ Part 2 (70 minutes)

You now have 70 minutes to review your notes and sources and to plan, draft, revise, and edit your essay. While you may use your notes and refer to the sources, your essay must represent your original work. You may refer to your responses to the questions in Part 1, but you cannot change those answers. Now read your assignment and the information about how your writing will be scored; then begin your work.

Your Assignment

It is time to start writing your argumentative essay. Remember, your essay should explain whether you agree or disagree with the idea that public-service workers should be allowed to strike. When writing your essay, find ways to use information from the three sources to support your argument. A good argumentative essay should include a strong claim, and it should address opposing arguments.

Argumentative Essay Scoring

Your essay will be scored using the following:

1. **Organization/purpose:** How well did you express your claim, address opposing claims, and support your claim with logical ideas? How well did your ideas flow from beginning to end? How effective was your introduction and conclusion?

2. **Evidence/elaboration:** How well did you incorporate relevant information from the sources? Did you use specific titles or numbers in referring to the sources? How strong is the elaboration for your ideas? Did you clearly state your ideas in your own words in a way that is appropriate for your audience and purpose?

3. **Conventions:** How well did you follow the rules of grammar, punctuation, capitalization, and spelling?

Now begin work on your essay. Manage your time carefully so that you can:

- plan your essay, using your notes
- write your essay
- revise and edit your final draft

RESEARCH SIMULATION

Informative Essay

You are a member of your school's ecology club, and club members have decided to write letters to newspapers about environmental issues. Your letters will be in the form of informative essays. You have chosen the topic of the water supply at the Everglades in Florida.

First you will review three articles about the water supply at Everglades National Park. After you have reviewed these sources, you will answer some questions about them. You should first skim the sources and the questions and then go back and read them carefully.

In Part 2, you will write an informative essay about the effects the water supply has on the Everglades.

Time Management: Informative Task

There are two parts to most formal writing tests. Both parts of the tests are timed, so it's important to use your limited time wisely.

Part 1: Read Sources and Answer Questions

Preview the Assignment

35 minutes

35 minutes! That's not much time.

You will have 35 minutes to read three articles about the effect of the water supply on Everglades National Park. You will also answer questions that will help you plan your essay.

How Many?

Preview the questions. This will help you know which information you'll need to find as you read.

How many pages of reading? ☐

How many multiple-choice questions? ☐

How many prose constructed-response questions? ☐

How do you plan to use the 35 minutes?

Underline, circle, and take notes as you read. You probably won't have time to reread.

This is a lot to do in a short time.

Estimated time to read:

Source #1: "Past and Present: The Florida Everglades" ☐ minutes

Source #2: "Can We Fix the Water Supply?" ☐ minutes

Source #3: "Water Quality Nearly Halts Everglades Restoration" ☐ minutes

Estimated time to answer questions? ☐ minutes

Total   **35 minutes**

Any concerns?

_____

_____

Part 2: Write the Essay

Plan and Write an Informative Essay

70 minutes

You will have 70 minutes to plan, write, revise, and edit your essay.

Your Plan

Before you start writing, determine the main idea of your essay and the details that support your main idea.

How do you plan to use the 70 minutes?

Estimated time for planning the essay?		minutes
Estimated time for writing?		minutes
Estimated time for editing?		minutes
Estimated time for checking spelling, grammar, and punctuation?		minutes
Total	**70**	**minutes**

Notes:

_____

_____

_____

_____

► Your Task

You are a member of your school's ecology club, and club members have decided to write letters to newspapers about environmental issues. Your letters will be in the form of informative essays. You have chosen the topic of the water supply at the Everglades in Florida. In researching the topic, you have identified three sources you will use in planning your informative essay.

After you have reviewed the sources, you will answer some questions about them. Briefly skim the sources and the three questions that follow. Then, go back and read the sources carefully so you will have the information you will need to answer the questions. Take notes on the sources as you read. You may refer back to your notes at any time during Part 1 or Part 2 of the performance task.

► Part 1 (35 minutes)

You will now read the sources. After carefully reading the sources, use the rest of the time in Part 1 to answer the three questions about them. Though your answers to these questions will help you think about what you have read and plan your essay, they will also be scored as part of the test.

SOURCE #1:

Past and Present:
The Florida Everglades

by Tobey Haskell

The Florida Everglades is a subtropical wilderness filled with grass marshes, hardwood hammocks (broad-leafed trees packed densely together that grow to be only a few inches tall), and mangrove forests. These wetlands were once the home to many rare, endangered, and exotic species. However, this is no longer the case due to changes in the environment. The Everglades have always existed in a delicate balance—even the smallest change can have a large impact.

Though the Seminole and Miccosukee tribes lived in the
10   Everglades prior to 1882, they did not attempt to alter the lush landscape. But when settlers from outside of Florida came to the Everglades, they considered it useless swampland. They had the idea of draining the Everglades.

From 1905–1910, the settlers began to convert the land so that it could be used for agricultural purposes. They laid rails for a railroad system, and more and more settlers came to the wetlands. The U.S. Army Corps of Engineers and government officials authorized the digging of canals, the creation of water storage facilities, and the regulation of the flow of water. The
20   streams were dredged, and the Everglades was nearly drained entirely.

The construction and population increase in the Everglades upset its fragile ecosystem, and cut off the flow of fresh water to the Everglades. As a result, the quantity and diversity of the wetlands' wildlife decreased and 50% of the original wetlands of South Florida no longer exist today.

Some people tried to defend and preserve the Everglades. In 1934, Congress designated the Everglades as a national park and in 1947 the park officially opened. The creation of the park
30   was a win for those who had worked toward protecting land in

NOTES

the area. However, they knew that changes to the land outside the park's boundary might create problems that would affect the land within the park.

In the 1960s, environmentalists came to the Everglades' aid, protesting the construction of an international airport in the area. From that time on, conservationists have been working to reverse the damage done to the wetlands by human actions.

Agribusinesses, government agencies, and conservation groups are working to restore Everglades National Park.
40 Improving and increasing the water supply is their first priority. Once a plan of action has been agreed on, the issue of money will come into play. How will the project be financed? Who will pay for it? The answers to these questions will determine what will become of the Everglades.

Am I on Track?

Actual Time Spent Reading

ANCHOR TEXT
SOURCE #2:
Can We Fix the Water Supply?

by Caleb Hughes

Imagine that, after a long afternoon spent working in the hot sun, you rush inside to pour yourself a nice, crisp glass of water. Upon turning on the faucet, nothing comes out. No bother, you'll just try another faucet in the house. Unfortunately, the water running from the other faucets in the house contains phosphorous, mercury, and other hazardous elements, making the water polluted and undrinkable. Does this sound like a nightmare?

This nightmare is a reality for one of our nation's most
10 beloved environmental treasures. Since 1900, drainage of the Everglades for development and farming has eroded the original wetlands by 50%. However, changes have been implemented to ensure that the Everglades will soon have access to all of the clean water that it and its millions of animal inhabitants need to survive.

The Everglades, which provides water to nearly 7 million people living in Florida, has fallen victim to three extended droughts over the last ten years. When a fragile ecosystem like the Everglades undergoes even a small change like a
20 particularly rainy storm or a short-term lapse in rainfall, the repercussions can be huge. Many animals and people rely on the Everglades' clean water supply as their primary source of water. When that water is in short supply or contaminated, the effects can be staggering.

One reason the water in the Everglades faces these issues is because the sugarcane crop grows so well there. The Everglades is host to 440,000 acres of sugar cane. As the demand for the sugarcane crop increases, more land is needed for planting, which means less land is available to support life. Also,
30 as the sugarcane crop is harvested, fertilizer used on the plants to ensure a successful crop introduces chemicals and excess amounts of nitrogen and phosphorus into the delicate

ecosystem. These chemicals contaminate the often limited water supply found in the Everglades.

Nonetheless, there is hope for the Everglades. A Supreme Court decision made in 2004 implemented an $8.4 billion project to re-establish the natural flow of water to the Everglades in the next 30 years. By making an effort to erase the effects of both nature and man on the Everglades, we are 40 working hard to ensure that this important part of Florida's landscape exists for many generations to come . . . and that all who call the Everglades home have access to plenty of clean, refreshing water!

Am I on Track?

Actual Time Spent Reading

SOURCE #3:
Water Quality Nearly Halts Everglades Restoration

by Robin Martelli

NOTES

The major obstacles to replenishing the water supply to the Everglades aren't related to construction or drought. The restoration of the Everglades is delayed because of the price tag and the quality of the water being sent to the wetlands.

In the early 20th century, the Everglades were drained to make the land agriculture-ready. It has been many years since the first settlers decided to alter the area. The water that once flowed into the Everglades is now directed to irrigate farmland and replenish supplies of urban drinking water.

10 We've come a long way since the early settlers began to drain the area. Plans are now in place to restore the Everglades by reinstituting the natural water flow to the wetlands that had previously been cut off. Unfortunately, the redirected water may not meet water quality standards.

The concern about the water quality stems from the amount of phosphorus present in the water. Phosphorous is found in fertilizer, decaying soil, and animal waste. In other words, it is likely to be present in areas around a farm. In 1986, when detrimental levels of phosphorous were discovered, water

20 management became a primary focus in the Everglades. This resulted in long court battles to determine who was responsible for the cleanup. As a result, the Everglades Forever Act was passed in 1994 by then-governor Lawton Chiles.

In 1999, a report on the health of the Everglades water system was drafted and submitted to Congress by the U.S. Army Corps of Engineers and the South Florida Water Management District. The report recommended improvements to the region that eventually led to the Comprehensive Everglades Restoration Plan (CERP), signed into law by

30 President Clinton in December of 2000. The cost of restoration was to be shared by the federal government and other sources.

But many were unhappy with the red tape and slow pace of CERP. In an attempt to accelerate much-needed assistance to the Central Everglades, the U.S. Army Corps of Engineers began an initiative called the Central Everglades Planning Project (CEPP). The new plan proposed to refill sections of manmade canals to help redirect some of the water that flows through them to the Everglades. The plan would also improve water quality by installing stormwater treatment marshes that

40 would act as filters for some of the pollution. Building more reservoirs in the Everglades would also address concerns about water quality.

The projected cost for the project is about $1 billion. Florida state leaders believe that the federal government should finance the project. However, federal funding would require congressional approval, something that might not be easy to attain.

In May of 2013, an encouraging solution emerged. A settlement between Florida's governor, the Obama

50 Administration, and the sugar industry has led to The Everglades Restoration Act, a bill that would invest $880 million in state money and restore water quality in the Everglades. This historic bill was approved unanimously by both the House and the Senate.

The Everglades Restoration Act will replace the final phase of the Everglades Forever Act introduced nearly two decades prior.

Am I on Track?

Actual Time Spent Reading

Part 1 Questions

Answer the following questions. You may refer to your reading notes, and you should cite text evidence in your responses. Your answers to these questions will be scored. You will be able to refer to your answers as you write your essay in Part 2.

1 **Prose Constructed-Response** What are two important problems with the water supply at Everglades National Park? Identify the problems, and support your answer with evidence from the three sources.

_____

_____

_____

_____

_____

_____

2 Based on the information in the sources, which of the following is an accurate statement?

   a. Humans are the only cause responsible for the problems in the Everglades.

   b. It is too late to save the Everglades from being destroyed.

   c. The Everglades ecosystem will be affected even if it is altered in a small way.

   d. The cost of saving the Everglades is the only issue delaying aid for the park.

3 Which evidence below **best** supports your answer to Question 2?

   a. "The projected cost for the project is about $1 billion." (Source #3)

   b. "Many animals and people rely on the Everglades' clean water supply as their primary source of water." (Source #2)

   c. "The concern about the water quality stems from the amount of phosphorus present in the water." (Source #3)

   d. "Agribusinesses, government agencies, and conservation groups are working to restore Everglades National Park." (Source #1)

► Part 2 (70 minutes)

You now have 70 minutes to review your notes and sources and to plan, draft, revise, and edit your essay. While you may use your notes and refer to the sources, your essay must represent your own original work. You may refer to your responses to the questions in Part 1, but you cannot change those answers. Now read your assignment and the information about how your writing will be scored; then begin your work.

Your Assignment

The ecology club has set a deadline for finishing its letter-writing campaign, and so it is time for you to begin writing your letter about the water supply in Everglades National Park. Your letter will be in the form of an informative essay. As you write your essay, make sure that you include information from the three sources and that you are presenting your ideas in a logical way.

Informative Essay Scoring

Your essay will be scored using the following:

1. **Organization/purpose:** How well did you state your thesis and support your thesis with a logical progression of ideas? Did you use a variety of transitions between ideas? Was your focus narrow enough to lead to a well-formed conclusion?

2. **Evidence/elaboration:** How well did you incorporate relevant information from the sources? How well did you elaborate your ideas? Did you use precise language appropriate to your audience and purpose?

3. **Conventions:** How well did you follow the rules of grammar, punctuation, capitalization, and spelling?

Now begin work on your essay. Manage your time carefully so that you can:

- plan your essay, using your notes
- write your essay
- revise and edit your final draft

TASK 3

Literary Analysis

Your language arts teacher has assigned your class a literary analysis of two poems. Both of these poems are about poetry itself.

First you will review the two poems. After you have reviewed these sources, you will answer some questions about them. You should first skim the sources and the questions and then go back and read them carefully.

In Part 2, you will write a literary analysis in which you compare and contrast the poems by Eve Merriam and Billy Collins.

Time Management: Literary Analysis Task

There are two parts to most formal writing tests. Both parts of the tests are timed, so it's important to use your limited time wisely.

Part 1: Read Sources and Answer Questions

35 minutes! That's not much time.

Preview the Assignment

35 minutes

You will have 35 minutes to read two poems to discover each writer's theme, or message. You will also answer questions that will help you plan your essay on the topic.

Preview the questions. This will help you know which information you'll need to find as you read.

How Many?

How many pages of reading?

How many multiple-choice questions?

How many prose constructed-response questions?

Underline, circle, and take notes as you read. You probably won't have time to reread.

How do you plan to use the 35 minutes?

This is a lot to do in a short time.

Estimated time to read:

    Source #1: "Inside a Poem" _____ minutes

    Source #2: "Introduction to Poetry" _____ minutes

Estimated time to answer questions? _____ minutes

Total   **35 minutes**

Any concerns?

_____

_____

_____

_____

Part 2: Write the Analysis

How much time do you have? Pay attention to the clock!

Plan and Write a Literary Analysis

→ **70 minutes**

You will have 70 minutes to plan, write, revise, and edit your literary analysis.

Your Plan

Before you start writing, decide how you will organize your literary analysis:

Point-by-Point? ☐   Subject-by-Subject? ☐

How do you plan to use the 70 minutes?

Be sure to leave enough time for this step.

Estimated time for planning the analysis?	☐ minutes
Estimated time for writing?	☐ minutes
→ Estimated time for editing?	☐ minutes
Estimated time for checking spelling, grammar, and punctuation?	☐ minutes
Total	**70 minutes**

Notes:

_____

_____

_____

_____

Reread your analysis, making sure that the points are clear. Check that there are no spelling or punctuation mistakes.

▶ Your Task

> Your language arts teacher has assigned a literary analysis to the class. You are to analyze two poems about poetry. You will work with these two sources to write an analysis that contrasts the themes, or messages about life, in each poem.

After you have reviewed the sources, you will answer some questions about them. Briefly skim the sources and the three questions that follow. Then, go back and read the sources carefully so you will have the information you will need to answer the questions. Take notes on the sources as you read. You may refer back to your notes at any time during Part 1 or Part 2 of the performance task.

▶ Part 1 (35 minutes)

You will now read the sources. After carefully reading the sources, use the rest of the time in Part 1 to answer the three questions about them. Though your answers to these questions will help you think about what you have read and plan your analysis, they will also be scored as part of the test.

SOURCE #1:
Inside a Poem

by Eve Merriam

© Houghton Mifflin Harcourt Publishing Company

It doesn't always have to rhyme,
but there's a repeat of a beat,
    somewhere
an inner chime that makes you want to
5 tap your feet or swerve in a curve;
a lilt, a leap, a lightning-split:—
thunderstruck the consonants jut,
while the vowels open wide as waves in
    the noon-blue sea.

10 You hear with your heels, your eyes feel
what they never touched before:
fins on a bird, feathers on a deer;
taste all colors, inhale
memory and tomorrow and always the
15   tang is today.

NOTES

Am I on Track?

Actual Time Spent Reading

Introduction to Poetry

by Billy Collins

NOTES

I ask them to take a poem
and hold it up to the light
like a color slide

or press an ear against its hive.

5 I say drop a mouse into a poem
and watch him probe his way out,

or walk inside the poem's room
and feel the walls for a light switch.

I want them to water-ski
10 across the surface of a poem
waving at the author's name on the shore.

But all they want to do
is tie the poem to a chair with rope
and torture a confession out of it.

15 They begin beating it with a hose
to find out what it really means.

Am I on Track?

Actual Time Spent Reading

Part 1 Questions

Answer the following questions. You may refer to your reading notes, and you should cite text evidence in your responses. Your answers to these questions will be scored. You will be able to refer to your answers as you write your essay in Part 2.

1 Which of the following sentences **best** states an important theme in both poems?

   a. It's important to keep an open mind when you read a poem.

   b. A poem can mean whatever you want it to mean.

   c. To find the true meaning of a poem, you need to use your sense of hearing.

   d. A good poem is usually difficult to understand.

2 Which of the following lines **best** supports the answer to Question 1?

   a. "It doesn't always have to rhyme . . . " (Source #1, line 1)

   b. " . . . thunderstruck the consonants jut, / while the vowels open wide as waves in / the noon-blue sea." (Source #1, lines 7–9)

   c. "I say drop a mouse into a poem / and watch him probe his way out . . . " (Source #2, lines 5–6)

   d. "They begin beating it with a hose / to find out what it really means." (Source #2, lines 15–16)

3 **Prose Constructed-Response** In Source #1, what do the images in lines 10–15 suggest about the way poetry affects readers?

_____

_____

_____

_____

_____

_____

▶ Part 2 (70 minutes)

You now have 70 minutes to review your notes and sources and to plan, draft, revise, and edit your essay. While you may use your notes and refer to the sources, your essay must represent your own original work. You may refer to your responses to the questions in Part 1, but you cannot change those answers. Now read your assignment and the information about how your writing will be scored; then begin your work.

Your Assignment

It's time to begin writing your literary analysis. Think about the two poems and what you want to say about them. As you write your essay, compare and contrast the themes, or messages about life, conveyed in the poems. Make sure that you include quotations from both poems and that you present your ideas in a logical order.

Literary Analysis Scoring

Your literary analysis will be scored using the following:

1. **Organization/purpose:** How well did you state your thesis/ controlling idea and support it with a logical progression of ideas? Did you use a variety of transitions between ideas? Was your controlling idea narrow enough to lead to a logical conclusion?

2. **Evidence/elaboration:** How well did you incorporate relevant information from the literary texts? How well did you elaborate your ideas? Did you use precise language appropriate to your audience and purpose?

3. **Conventions:** How well did you follow the rules of grammar, punctuation, capitalization, and spelling?

Now begin work on your essay. Manage your time carefully so that you can:

- plan your essay, using your notes
- write your essay
- revise and edit your final draft

© Houghton Mifflin Harcourt Publishing Company

Acknowledgments

"Abuelito Who" from *My Wicked Wicked Ways* by Sandra Cisneros. Text copyright © 1987 by Sandra Cisneros. Published by Third Woman Press and in hardcover by Alfred A. Knopf. Reprinted by permission of Susan Bergholz Literary Services, New York, NY and Lamy, NM. All rights reserved.

"Goodbye Food Pyramid, Hello Dinner Plate" (Retitled: "The Food Pyramid and Why It Changed") by William Neuman from *The New York Times,* May 27, 2011. Text copyright © 2011 by The New York Times. Reprinted by permission of PARS International on behalf of The New York Times.

"The Half-Life of Facts" (Retitled: "Half-Life of Science Facts") by Samuel Arbesman and Charles Babbage from *The Economist,* November 28, 2012. Text copyright © 2012 by The Economist. Reprinted by permission of The Economist Newspaper Ltd.

"Helicopter Rescues Increasing On Everest" interview with Nick Heil by Robert Siegel from *National Public Radio,* May 23, 2012, www.npr.org. Text copyright © 2012 by National Public Radio. Reprinted by permission of National Public Radio.

"Inside a Poem" from *It Doesn't Always Have to Rhyme* by Eve Merriam. Text copyright © 1964 by Eve Merriam. Reprinted by permission of Marian Reiner Literary Agency.

"Introduction to Poetry" from *The Apple that Astonished Paris* by Billy Collins. Text copyright © 1998 by Billy Collins. Reprinted by permission of The Permissions Company on behalf of University of Arkansas Press.

Excerpt from "New York School Bus Strike—Sign of National Pressure on Unions" by Stacy Teicher Khadaroo from *The Christian Science Monitor,* January 18, 2013. Text copyright © 2013 by The Christian Science Monitor. Reprinted by permission of The Christian Science Publishing Society.

Excerpt from "The Old Grandfather and His Little Grandson" from *Twenty-Two Russian Tales for Young Children* by Leo Tolstoy. Text copyright © 1969 by Miriam Morton. Reprinted by permission of Simon & Schuster, Inc.

"Ranger Killed During Rescue of Climbers on Mount Rainier" by Alexa Vaughn from *The Seattle Times,* June 21, 2012. Text copyright © 2012 by The Seattle Times. Reprinted by permission of The Seattle Times.

"Stopping by Woods on a Snowy Evening" from *The Poetry of Robert Frost* by Robert Frost. Text copyright © 1969 by Holt, Rinehart and Winston, Inc. Reprinted by permission of Henry Holt & Company.